BE SMART
PAY
ZERO
TAXES

USE THE BUY, BORROW, DIE STRATEGY TO GET RICH AND STAY RICH

MARK J. QUANN

Humanix Books

www.humanixbooks.com

This book is dedicated to the working man—the average American who goes to work each day and pays his taxes. It is for those who have labored in factories and on assembly lines, building the very fabric of our country. To the HVAC workers, carpet cleaners, plumbers, electricians, and roofers, and to those who build chimneys and fireplaces. This book is for all who have mixed concrete under the hot sun or spent weeks drilling concrete in the dirt beneath houses. It is dedicated to the security guards, private investigators, and the kids who didn't like school and dropped out of college.

I can relate. I'm one of you.

—Mark

Contents

Part One: Stocks and ETFs

Part Three: Income and Asset Protection

Part Four: Cryptocurrency

Part Five: Precious Metals

Part Six: Business Ownership

The Solid Foundation of a Buy, Borrow, Die Strategy   235

Part Seven: Advanced Concepts

Improving the Performance of a Buy, Borrow, Die Strategy   271

Author's Note: Finding My Purpose

To this day, it surprises me that I became an author of three books about money.

I didn't plan to write another book, but my friends thought I had found "the secret" to building wealth and paying no taxes, and they thought it was vitally important to share it.

I'll assume that you are not familiar with my story, and the story of how I became an author. But during the process, I found my purpose: to educate others about how money *really* works, and create lasting, transformative change that will ripple through generations.

This book is dual-purpose: It will teach you a simple but very effective tax strategy to help you achieve financial independence. And when you achieve financial independence, I hope you also find *your* purpose.

This book will be the foundation for every student and teacher in future classes of The Perfect Portfolio™ course—because I know its content is that powerful.

A Note to Financial Advisors

My goal is not to have all my readers fire their financial advisors. Remember, *I was one of you*.

I spent 15 years sitting across a kitchen table helping families implement strategies to save and invest.

I also believed I was doing the best for my clients . . . and I was . . . *with the knowledge and products that I had access to*.

If you are financial advisor, I hope this book also helps you achieve financial freedom (at any age), and I hope you *use the knowledge you now have gained* to help others do the same.

1

The Pandemic Epiphany

How I Discovered The Perfect Portfolio™

> **per·fect**
> /ˈpərfək(t)/
> *adjective*
> having all the required or desirable elements, qualities,
> or characteristics; as good as it is possible to be
>
> **port·fo·li·o**
> /pôrtˈfōlēō/
> *noun*
> a range of investments held by a person or organization

It was January 2020, and all my speaking engagements had been canceled because of the COVID-19 pandemic. The stock market was crashing, and I found myself walking around the pool pondering how I would spend my time in 2020.

The government was handing out free money—no taxes, no strings attached. I was concerned about the inflation that would follow, and I made a post on Instagram encouraging others to invest the "free money," rather than spending it. Then a friend asked me a question: "Mark, why don't you start a financial education company?" I had been teaching finances for over a decade and I loved the idea!

Some friends and I got together, and we began brainstorming. We knew we wanted to build a financial education company that would benefit everyone, regardless of their income or level of financial education. Soon I was consumed in writing and developing a curriculum for the course, and I found my inspiration to write my third book. It was then that I wrote down the following: **"The #1 rule in my investing is simple: If I can't use OPM [other people's money] to invest, it is not a good investment. PERIOD. No Exceptions."** I didn't know it at the time, but it became a guiding principle for the next three years and a staple of all my investing.

We began teaching the tax strategies I had covered in *Top 10 Ways to Avoid Taxes*, but we found that we could take these strategies to the next level by buying assets and then borrowing against them—completely tax-free—to buy more assets.

We defined the three goals that would be attainable for all our students.

The Perfect Portfolio would:

1. "Raise Your Financial IQ"
2. "Teach You to Fish"
3. And "Automate Your Income™" (which we now own the trademark to!)

We named the course The Perfect Portfolio. But . . . what strategy would we use to build The Perfect Portfolio? Then it appeared!

It was July 2021 when I found THE strategy.

I was reading the *Wall Street Journal* when I stumbled on an article called "Buy, Borrow, Die: How Rich Americans Live off Their Paper Wealth." The article talked about how "the wealthy are borrowing more than ever, using low-interest loans backed by their investments."

Why had I never heard of this strategy?

I began a deep dive, and here is what I learned: The term "Buy, Borrow, Die" was coined by University of Southern California tax law professor Edward McCaffery in the 1990s as a simple way to explain how the ultra-wealthy avoid paying taxes. And yes, many pay NO TAXES at all. The article mentioned how the wealthy buy assets and never sell them and never pay taxes. Rather than sell the assets (and trigger the taxes), they simply take loans, which are 100% tax-free.

Let's give you a basic example:

Imagine you buy a stock for $1,000. Over the years, it grows to $10,000. Instead of selling it and paying (capital gains) tax on the $9,000 profit, you borrow $5,000 against it, which you use to purchase another $5,000 of stock. You avoided paying taxes because you didn't sell, and you are now investing a total of $15,000—and you only paid taxes on the money you originally earned to buy that first $1,000 of stock.

As each asset grows in value, you repeat the process of buying and borrowing against each asset to purchase additional assets, thus avoiding paying any taxes. Sounds simple, doesn't it?

I can hear the screams already: "But what about Dave Ramsey? Aren't we supposed to get out of debt?"

I love Dave, but he has never said, "I will teach you how to get super-wealthy and Pay No Taxes."

But I will.

> **"Ordinary people don't think about debt the way billionaires think about debt."**
>
> —Edward McCaffery,
> University of Southern California
> Gould School of Law

No portfolio is going to be right for everyone. The key is to decide what's right for you and build *YOUR* Perfect Portfolio.

2

Be S.M.A.R.T.

Strategies to Maximize Assets and Reduce Taxes

smart

/smärt/

adjective

having or showing a quick-witted intelligence

There are lots of smart people in the world, and being smart does have its advantages. IQ does play a role in how much money you make, but the good news is that it will not be the deciding factor defining your success—and if you become rich or if you become poor. I was never the smartest guy in the class, and there were always other students with a higher IQ, but I was smart enough to discover a simple formula that I've used to get where I am today:

- First I DECIDE where I want to be in the future.
- Then I find people that are where I want to be and follow their advice.

- Finally, I outwork everyone else until I reach my goal.

If you doubt it's that simple, let me give you an example: I'm a high school and college dropout that hated school and reading, but I'm also an author and I sell a lot of books. According to the Amazon reviews, 9 out of 10 people who read my books really love them.

To show what I mean, here are some summaries of the reviews of my first three books, helpfully generated by the online retailer's AI helper bot:

- *Rich Man, Poor Bank*
  "Customers find the book very informative, **easy to understand**, and **quick to read**. They also describe it as a quick and dirty financial ed." ("quick and dirty," lol)
- *Top 10 Ways to Avoid Taxes*
  "Customers find the book adds nuggets of practical knowledge and a nice glossary of tax terms. They also say it provides **simple** ways to make money easily and great tools that work. Readers say the book looks like an **easy read**."
- *Top 25 Ways an IUL Can Secure Your Financial Future*
  "Customers find the book very informative and **easy to understand**. They also say the strategies are key to financial freedom."

You will notice a common theme in the reviews: "simple," "easy to understand," and "easy read." That is the biggest compliment I can get as an author of financial books.

The negative reviews are the "smart/negative" (or both) people that already know everything (or, at least, think that they do). I wish them the best, truly.

So here are my goals as you read this book:

- **I hope the reviews for this book are similar to those for my earlier books.** An "easy read" and "simple and easy to understand." Nothing would make me happier, other than hearing about the success that readers have after reading this book.
- **I hope that every chapter of this book is worth the cost of the book.** (I believe that it was Tim Ferris, author of *The 4-Hour Workweek*, who said that on his blog). If you paid $25 for this book, I hope that every chapter can either make you $25, save you (in taxes) at least $25, or both. I believe it can make you millions—and save you millions in taxes too!
- **I hope that this book will change your thinking.** Teacher, yoga instructor, and author Sahdguru once said, "Thinking is just a recycling of the data you have gathered in the past." Take a moment and think about that. That alone can make you $25, and it can also change your entire life ... but only if you THINK about it and put those thoughts to work. (Thinking about wealth, and changing your mindset, can be one of the hardest hurdles for a lot of people when it comes to making long-term positive change. You've got to get out of the mindset that so many folks have, as shown in Figure 2-1.)

So have you decided where you want to be in the future? Is your goal financial freedom and paying no taxes? If so, the next step is to find people who have already achieved that and follow their advice. Are your current advisors teaching you to build

FIGURE 2-1 It's not all "THEIRS"; it's yours, and you've got the right to keep as much of it as possible.

wealth, retire early, and pass all that wealth to your family—all without paying taxes?

If not, ask yourself these questions:

- "Is my CPA financially free because of smart investing, and is my CPA showing me how to pay no taxes?"
- "Are my financial advisors financially independent due to their investments, and have they shown me a clear path to an early and tax-free retirement that mirrors theirs?"

And if you are one of our younger readers heading to college for business or finance, look for a class called "How to Get Wealthy at a Young Age and Pay No Taxes." If it's not offered, before you sign those student loans, ask yourself, "Where does the financial education taught at colleges and universities come from, and who really benefits from what they're going to teach me?"

It's up to you to think about your answers and decide where you want to be in the future . . .

We're going to extensively cover "Strategies to Maximize Assets and Reduce Taxes"—in short, S.M.A.R.T.—and show you a path toward retirement at any age. But let's not forget the lessons from *Rich Dad Poor Dad*. "An asset is something that puts money in your pocket," and a liability is "something that takes money out of your pocket."

It is important that you buy assets and avoid liabilities.

Now, with that in mind, I will teach you the most powerful, simplest, and most universal tax strategy that anyone can use to PAY ZERO TAXES!

Master the language of money, and seek mentors who speak it fluently.

3

What Is Money?

Is a Cow Money?

> **mon·ey**
>
> /ˈmənē/
>
> *noun*
>
> something generally accepted as a medium of exchange, a measure of value, or a means of payment

If you've been told that money is that paper or those coins in your wallet, you've been lied to.

There was a time that it was easy to identify money. If you held a nickel, a dime, or a quarter in your hand, it was made of a precious metal such as silver or gold. The paper money in your wallet was backed by a commodity (in the United States our money was backed by silver from 1792 to 1834 and then by gold from 1834 until 1971); those precious metals gave the paper value because there was a **limited supply** of the precious metals.

Today, almost all the currency in the world is known as "fiat currency." The term "fiat" is derived from Latin, meaning "Let it be done" or "Let it be." In the context of currency, "fiat" refers to an authoritative or arbitrary order. Therefore, fiat currency is money that has value because the government has declared it to be legal tender, regardless of it's true value *before* they printed a number on it. For example, one piece of paper says, "ONE DOLLAR," and another says, "ONE HUNDRED DOLLARS." They're both printed on the same paper, using the same ink, and they're the same size, so why is one worth 100 times more than the other?

Fiat currency is a type of money that is issued by a government and that only has value because the government maintains it **and because the people have faith in its value**. Unlike commodity money (which is backed by a physical good like gold or silver), fiat currency has no intrinsic value and is not backed by a physical commodity. Instead, its value is derived from the trust and confidence that people have in the issuing government and its ability to maintain the currency's stability. Almost every currency in the world today is an example of fiat currency. (There are very few notable exceptions: Zimbabwe, for example, now has a gold-backed currency, the ZiG, which it introduced in April 2024 in response to hyperinflation in the country.)

So let's take a moment to recap the lessons learned before we go deeper down this rabbit hole. The fiat currency in your wallet is backed only by the belief of the people that it is worth something. The nickels, dimes, and quarters are made of worthless metals. I know why colleges and universities don't offer any classes called "The History of Money: From Gold and Silver to Fiat and the Future of the US Dollar." (*Hint:* If they taught that class, there'd be a lot of angry college students . . .)

Now, if they did offer such a class, it would certainly teach you about "fractional reserve banking." I covered the basics of fractional reserve banking in *Rich Man, Poor Bank*, but let's review the basics.

Fractional reserve banking is a banking system in which banks are required to keep only a small fraction of their depositors' funds in reserve, either in the bank's vaults or at the central bank. The rest of the deposits can be loaned out to borrowers. This system allows banks to create money through lending, thereby increasing the money supply. It relies on the assumption (and hope, which isn't exactly solid fiscal policy) that not all depositors will withdraw their funds at the same time.

Here is an example of how the banks use fractional reserve banking to expand the money supply:

You deposit $1,000 in Bank A.

The bank is only required to keep 10% of deposits as reserves. So Bank A keeps $100 in reserve and can loan out $900. I know, that sounds crazy, doesn't it? But that is just the beginning of the cycle of money creation.

Bank A loans $900 to another person, who then deposits this $900 in Bank B.

Bank B keeps 10% of the $900 ($90) in reserve and loans out $810.

The process continues with each subsequent bank keeping 10% of the new deposit in reserve and loaning out the rest.

Through this process the initial $1,000 deposit can lead to a total increase in the money supply far exceeding the original amount deposited, because the same money is counted multiple times in the system as it gets loaned out and redeposited. This is how fractional reserve banking **expands the money supply**.

What's important to understand is that when the money supply expands, most of the money in circulation is created as debt—virtually, in a computer. Money is created and destroyed with the push of a button.

This is when you should be asking, "When new money is created, who gets a cut?" Great question!

Let's say you buy an LG TV at Costco. LG makes a profit—that's fair; after all, it provided value and jobs and helped lower the price of TVs.

Costco also makes a profit—again, that's fair; it provided value and jobs and kept prices competitive.

And yes, a megabank collects a swipe fee—that's fair; it provided value and jobs too.

But here's the kicker: The city, state, and federal governments also take a cut through sales taxes—on top of all the taxes on manufacturing, storage, shipping, and more. There are import taxes, gasoline taxes, property taxes on the buildings, corporate taxes, employment taxes, income taxes on the companies and on all their employees, and so on—all of which get passed on to you when you swipe your credit card.

Here's another example of how money is created—this time when buying a home:

Let's say you buy a $400,000 home with just 3% down. For simplicity, we'll assume the $12,000 down payment is physical cash (though it's really just another bank entry), and the remaining $388,000 is created as debt in a computer—a simple bank entry with a few clicks of a keyboard.

That $388,000 is used to buy the home. As interest accrues, the bank just logs more entries—profit for the bank.

So, what happens if someone forecloses on a home? Another great question.

The bank simply deletes the entry.

I know what you're thinking: "Wait, the bank just creates an entry for my mortgage, then adds more entries for the interest on my debt? That sounds terrible!"

Yes, it might sound horrible, but here's the thing—you didn't pay any taxes on the borrowed money, did you? That $388,000 was created in a computer to buy your home, and it's 100% tax-free.

Now, ask yourself:

Do you want to work hard, pay taxes, and try to save $388,000 in after-tax money over many years while battling inflation?

Or . . .

Would you rather sign a mortgage and instantly create that $388,000, which is completely tax-free?

As of 2024, there's about $2.3 trillion of physical money in circulation. But when you include all the bank entries—what's called the "broad" money supply—it totals around $21 trillion. That means the broad money supply is roughly 10 times the physical money supply.

We've all been told to go to school, work hard, and pay taxes, but we've only been taught how to use debt in ways that make banks, corporations, and other families wealthy.

Isn't it time you learned to use debt to make your own family wealthy?

To fully understand how to use debt, or OPM (other people's money), to make your family wealthy, you'll need to keep reading and studying the following pages. But remember, you must continue to study, raise your financial IQ, and never stop learning.

DEFINING WHAT MONEY REALLY IS

First, let's identify what money really is by looking at its key characteristics:

1. Enough people **agree it has value**.
2. It must be **easily transferable**.
3. It must be in **limited supply**.

So how do you identify money?

Is a cow money?

You might be thinking, "No, a cow is a cow." And you'd be right—but it's important to look back in history. Money has taken many forms, and there was a time when a piece of paper (or, historically speaking, a clay tablet) was just an IOU for cows, which gave the paper value. That "worthless piece of paper" became money simply because there was a limited supply of cows backing it. (See Figure 3-1.)

FIGURE 3-1 Is a cow moo-lah?

Now, is the ONE DOLLAR silver coin I'm holding in my hand money? Yes or no? Well, yes, it is. But is it only worth $1?

Obviously, it's worth a lot more in today's dollars because it's made of silver. The silver in that coin is worth about $29 today. Pretty cool, right? Well, it is if you own silver coins.

What should concern you is that the price of silver was about $18 in 2019. This means paper money is rapidly losing its value—in relation to anything with a limited supply, like silver, gold, and, yes, cows.

But there's another lesson to learn from this silver coin. This ONE DOLLAR coin was created in 1888, and it's worth about $60 today. It's 90% silver, and there is a limited supply of them because it's impossible to create more silver coins from 1888. (Unless you have a time machine, in which case, forget silver coins—you've got lottery numbers to memorize and future stock tips to cash in on!)

Let me give you one more example when looking at our paper money:

I'm holding two ONE DOLLAR bills in my hands.

The first one, in my left hand, was created in 1987. It says "UNITED STATES OF AMERICA" near the top and "ONE DOLLAR" on the bottom. The statement "THIS NOTE IS LEGAL TENDER FOR ALL DEBTS, PUBLIC AND PRIVATE" is displayed in small font, and the term "FEDERAL RESERVE NOTE" is written at the top.

In my right hand, I'm holding a $1 bill created in 1935. It says "UNITED STATES OF AMERICA" near the top and "ONE DOLLAR" on the bottom. "THIS NOTE IS LEGAL TENDER FOR ALL DEBTS, PUBLIC AND PRIVATE" is displayed in small font, but the most important difference is that it displays the words "SILVER CERTIFICATE" at the top. As they say, the devil is in the details.

We had real money until August 1971, when President Nixon took us off the gold standard. That's when our money became fiat currency. I prefer the term "fake" money.

What's shocking is how fast Federal Reserve Notes have lost their value since 1971. According to www.in2013dollars. com, the value of our fiat currency has lost 87% of its purchasing power.

Let's look at inflation since August 1971 when it was around 4.6%. (And that was the actual inflation rate, unlike the current "inflation rate," which has been watered down to not include the food and energy sectors, which are the things actually impacted most by inflation. If you've recently bought gas for your car or food for your family, you know how much the prices of those items have shot up, and yet they're not in the officially reported inflation numbers you see on TV or read in the papers.)

Starting in 1972, inflation ramped up again and soon spiraled out of control. By April 1980, it had soared to 14.76%. In response, the Federal Reserve raised the Fed Funds rate—the rate banks charge each other for lending money—to a staggering 19%. This aggressive move eventually worked, and by 1987, inflation had fallen to just 3.66%.

That got me thinking . . . what could you buy for $1 in 1987?

$1 could get you more than a gallon of gasoline. Today, the average cost of gasoline is $3.15. That's more than 235% inflation.

A $1 bill could have bought two loaves of bread. Today, you need about $3 to get one loaf of bread. That's more than 500% inflation.

The average cost of a home was $104,500. Today, that same home costs about $495,000. More than 370% inflation.

So in 2024, what's the government's plan to tame inflation?

It's the same plan as in 1987, 1997, 2007, and 2017. It will print more money, give it away (to buy votes), and reduce interest rates to "stimulate" the economy. Sounds reasonable, right?

Okay, back to the question: "What is money?"

Money is anything that enough people agree has value, it must be easily transferable, and it must be in limited supply.

Above all, remember:

Anything in unlimited supply will go down in value.

And . . .

Anything with a limited supply will go up in value.

The unfortunate truth is that the Federal Reserve has been on this drunken spiral of monetary policy for far too long. There's a loss of public trust, and the repeated cycles have resulted in massive income inequality, with inflation stealing from the poor and giving to the rich.

As they say, the first step to recovery is realizing there's a problem.

So I leave you with two choices:

You can "create money" to buy cars and TVs—to make others wealthy.

Or . . .

You can learn to create (tax-free) money—to build your wealth.

Which one sounds better to you?

Money can be made using debt, and debt is tax-free. "Make" money to build your wealth.

4

The Millionaire
Next Door

Joe's Journey to $6 Million by Never Selling

> **mil·lion·aire**
>
> /ˌmilyəˈner, ˈmilyəˌner/
>
> *noun*
>
> a person whose assets are worth $1 million or more

N ow, let's prove to you that anyone can "create money." Meet Joe.

Joe was 26 years old and had a job, a wife and two kids, and a white picket fence. He went to church on Sundays, liked to buy stocks using his iPhone, and had read a few books about money and investing. Like any good investor, Joe had read *The Money Makeover* by Dave Ramsey and *Rich Dad Poor Dad* by Robert Kiyosaki. Joe didn't have a crystal ball to pick stocks. In fact, anyone could have done what Joe did; it was very "average." Let's see if Joe can do better than average.

It was 2004, and Joe had been told by a coworker, "Only buy the stocks of the companies that you use in your daily life," and so he decided to start with just $1,000 to buy Apple stock. He also set automatic investments to purchase additional Apple shares, auto-investing an additional $500 a month. Joe didn't worry about his account value; the idea was to just keep buying every month, regardless of the ups and downs of the market. This is called "dollar-cost averaging," and you will be buying more shares in down markets. He rode the ups and downs of the market and accumulated more shares through the Great Recession.

By 2014, Joe had $496,731 of Apple stock. Joe knew that if he never sold it, it would continue to grow with no taxes. Joe calculated that he had invested (and paid taxes on) roughly $60,000.

"Wow," he said to himself, "I'm 36, and I've got almost $500,000 in my stock account!" It seemed unbelievable for anyone, but especially for someone so average.

Joe found himself thinking . . . "What should I buy now?" Joe also used Microsoft products every day, and so he decided, "I'll buy $25,000 of Microsoft, but this time I'll double down and invest $1,000 every month to purchase additional Microsoft shares." Then Joe had a very *unaverage* thought: "What if I used my margin account to buy the $25,000 of Microsoft stock and also set up an auto-buy of $1,000 a month, also using my margin?"

Joe was a little uncertain, so first he wanted to check with "Dave" and "Robert." He Googled, "Should I take a margin loan to buy stocks?"

Dave's advice was as follows:

Unfortunately, there are a lot of financial "experts" out there who want you to use debt to get rich. They'll use smoke and mirrors and throw around fancy terms like "leverage" and "margin" to make this sound like a sophisticated investing strategy that will put you on the fast track to a high net worth. But the reality is this: Taking on debt in order to invest is riskier than climbing a mountain without a rope.

"Climbing a mountain without a rope!?" thought Joe. "That sounds scary, and average people don't climb mountains without a rope! In fact, they don't climb mountains at all."
Now, what would Robert say?

Buying stock on margin lets you leverage your funds much like a real estate investor uses a bank loan. Embracing Rich Dad's philosophy means using debt wisely after you're educated, not before. Leveraging money with "good debt" is a practice to respect, not fear—unlike the kind of debt that chains you to a job.

Robert also stated:

We often say debt is a lot like a loaded gun. If you use it without training and education, terrible things can happen. If you use it correctly and with your education, it can be a great tool.

Joe decided to continue investing $500 a month to purchase additional Apple shares, but he would take a margin loan to buy

$25,000 of Microsoft stock, plus purchase an additional $1,000 of stock a month, also using margin.

He continued buying and borrowing to purchase Microsoft stock, even during the roller-coaster ride of the pandemic.

Joe's buying and borrowing paid off, as by August of 2024, Joe had over $5,233,312 worth of Apple stock, plus his Microsoft shares were worth $912,450.

After making a few calculations, he came to a shocking conclusion: "I've got over $6,145,762 in stock, but I've only had to earn and pay taxes on $120,000!" Assuming a 28% tax bracket, Joe had paid $33,600 in taxes and now had a net worth of over $6 million.

Joe was no longer "Average" Joe. He had stumbled across "buying" and "borrowing" to build wealth tax-free.

As I'm writing this today, we don't know what the future will hold, but what if (now wealthy) Joe decided to double down once again, and this time borrow $25,000 to buy Amazon stock, and borrow $25,000 to buy Alphabet (Google), and borrow on margin to buy another $1,000 per month of each?

And . . . what if Joe decided to also apply this same strategy to buy real estate?

If you decide to use debt to build tax-free wealth, only take advice from sophisticated investors who have done it themselves.

5

Avoiding "Dead Money"

Invest in The Five Pillars That Can Secure Loans

> **dead**
>
> /ded/
>
> *adjective*
>
> (of a piece of equipment) no longer functioning

Awesome, you're still reading! I can imagine some of the many reactions so far, and fully expect a few angry emails: "Dave was right, and you are wrong!" and "You have to get out of debt to become financially free!"

It's a free country. Decide what is best for you.

But for those that are still here, I'm assuming that you are enjoying the descent down the rabbit hole of buying and borrowing to acquire assets? It is a very deep hole (see Figure 5-1), but I assure you, it is worth it. And it is better than working hard and paying endless taxes.

FIGURE 5-1   Down the finance rabbit hole. There's no turning back!

In my first book, *Rich Man, Poor Bank*, I defined "lazy money" as the money that sits idle at your megabank, likely earning 0.01%, minus the fees (and minus the taxes). Yes, it is important to put all your lazy money to work, earning the highest rates possible until it is put to work. The important part to remember is that "lazy money" is also taxed at the highest rates. 5%, less the taxes is likely closer to 3%. Minus 3–4% for inflation, and you are back to where you started.

Now, let's identify if you are killing your money. I define "dead money" as any money invested that you cannot use to take a loan *secured by* that investment.

For the remainder of this book, we will show you how to buy and borrow secured by five assets:

1. Stocks and ETFs
2. Real estate
3. Life insurance
4. Cryptocurrency
5. Gold and precious metals

We call these "The Five Pillars" of the Buy, Borrow, Die strategy—with the ultimate goal of paying zero taxes.

Why do we call these five asset classes "The Five Pillars" of the Buy, Borrow, Die strategy? Think of these as the support beams in your financial house of dreams. Each one carries its own weight and plays a critical role in building a fortress of wealth that, fingers crossed, the taxman can't penetrate.

Another way to think of them is as the Avengers of the financial world—each brings a unique superpower to the team, and they all work together to fight the evil nemesis: taxes (feel free to "boo" the evil villain). Just as you wouldn't want to rely on just one superhero to save the day, each of these assets plays a crucial role in building and protecting your wealth fortress.

First up, stocks and ETFs—they're like the Iron Man of your portfolio. Suave, sophisticated, and ready to soar, they provide the liquidity and flexibility needed to secure loans faster than you can say "bull market."

And then there's real estate, the Captain America, standing strong through economic ups and downs, providing solid ground to leverage against.

Life insurance? That's your Thor, wielding Mjolnir to smash through estate taxes and leaving a financial legacy as mighty as the God of Thunder himself.

Cryptocurrency—the newest team member—is a bit like Spider-Man swinging into the scene with youthful energy and sky-high potential. This digital asset might be the rookie, but it packs a punch with its rapid growth and high ceiling for wealth accumulation.

Last (but definitely not least), precious metals like gold are the Hulk—seemingly calm, but when inflation hits, they can smash through economic instability, offering a safe haven when the financial world goes green with envy at your savvy.

Together, these Five Pillars support more than just a strategy; they're the backbone of a smart, tax-efficient plan that uses borrowing to your advantage and keeps your wealth well protected. By *borrowing against* these assets instead of selling them, you keep the taxman at bay—making sure that your wealth grows, your family thrives, and you have a bit of fun watching your investments work smarter, not harder.

 Don't kill your money.

6

Financial Alchemy

How to Transform "Bad Debt" into "Good Debt"

> **al·che·my**
>
> /ˈalkəmē/
>
> *noun*
>
> a process that is so effective that it seems like magic, such as the transformation of base metals into gold

When Jane inquired about The Perfect Portfolio course, she had already watched some YouTube videos about the Buy, Borrow, Die strategy. I decided to meet with her on Zoom to see how I could help.

She let me know that she wanted to pay less taxes, but that was not her main or immediate concern. She told me her story: "When my mother got sick, I had to take time off work to care for her, and because of that I've accumulated around $22,000 of credit card debt, at around 24–28% interest. I'm currently paying $950 a month and about $450 a month is going to interest."

I mentioned that our first goal was to eliminate bad debt, with the top priority being to pay off all her credit cards.

Upon completing a review of her assets, I saw she had about $52,000 in the Vanguard ETF, VOO, held at one of the mega brokers. Before Jane and I had talked, she had called her financial advisor and was told that the best way get rid of the debt was to "liquidate [her] ETFs to pay off [her] credit card debt." Her financial advisor continued, "You'll be free of the credit card debt, but you will also have to pay the taxes from selling the shares."

I let Jane know there was a much better option. I explained, "Your broker charges around 14% interest for a margin loan, but you can transfer your ETFs, tax-free, to M1 Finance or Robinhood, both of which offer margin loans at around 6–7% [current rates as of late 2024]."

I guided her through completing the online ACATS (Automated Customer Account Transfer Service) form, and her ETF shares arrived at the new broker the following week. Once the transfer was complete, Jane took a $22,000 margin loan, which was deposited directly into her bank account. She then used the funds to pay off her credit card debt.

Once the transfer was complete, Jane pressed the Borrow button and was able to take a $22,000 margin loan and used it to pay off her credit card debt.

She didn't liquidate her shares, so she didn't trigger any taxes, and we had eliminated her 24–28% credit card debt with a loan at 6.25% interest. Doesn't that sound like a much better option to you? And even better, since the loan was secured by her ETF shares, she still earns any potential growth and/or dividends from her ETFs too!

"Jane," I said, "now that you're free of your high-interest debt, start taking the $950 you were paying toward the credit cards, and use it instead to invest and purchase additional ETFs. If you keep that $52,000 of VOO and invest the additional $950 each month for the next five years, and if we assume 10% growth per year, you'd have almost $160,000 in your account."

Jane was shocked, and she learned an incredibly valuable lesson that buying and borrowing can also be used to eliminate "bad debt" and replace it with "good debt," while also avoiding the taxes from selling her shares.

In a later chapter we will cover Jane's journey to learning the Buy, Borrow, Die strategy as well as the steps she took to build all Five Pillars—and strengthen the Pillars when buying and borrowing.

Selling assets triggers the taxes and kills the assets.

Never sell your assets, and always buy more.

PART ONE

Stocks and ETFs

*The First Pillar of a Buy,
Borrow, Die Strategy*

The Five Pillars

7

Buy Low and Never Sell

Stocks and ETFs,
the First Pillar of Buy, Borrow, Die

> **ac·cu·mu·late**
>
> /əˈkyoōm(y)ə lāt/
>
> *noun*
>
> the practice of collecting and gathering something (such as money)

As a "fiduciary" financial advisor and investment advisor representative (IAR) for over a decade, I helped my clients open hundreds of mutual funds, IRAs (individual retirement accounts), Roth IRAs, 529 (college saving) plans, 401(k) plans, etc. "We will set you up a diversified portfolio of mutual funds" was the cookie-cutter advice I gave them.

This theme could be repeated in a number of ways:

- "You want a Roth IRA? We will put you in a diversified portfolio of mutual funds."

- "You want a retirement account? We will put you in a diversified portfolio of mutual funds."
- "Need a 529 plan for the kids? We will put you in a diversified portfolio of mutual funds."

When I couldn't say the words "diversified portfolio of mutual funds" without a gag reflex, I knew it was time to resign from giving traditional "financial advice."

Today, I invest very differently in my personal brokerage account than how I was taught to invest as a financial advisor. In fact, if a financial advisor recommended the strategies that I personally use, that advisor would very likely be fired—for what the industry refers to as "selling away." "Selling away" is a practice in the financial industry where a financial advisor or broker recommends or facilitates the sale of investment products that have not been approved by their broker-dealer. This can be a good thing, as we don't want financial advisors recommending investments that may be too risky for their client or may be too complicated for the client to understand. But this also restricts your financial advisor from being totally honest with you. Financial advisors might personally invest in individual stocks using the Buy, Borrow, Die strategy, but they are selling you a diversified portfolio of mutual funds in your IRA that will hammer you in taxes when you retire. Okay, this is also highly unlikely . . . as most financial advisors don't understand the Buy, Borrow, Die strategy, or how to implement it, but you get my point.

I want to be clear that I'm also not bashing on financial advisors. After all, I was one of them myself! And I did the best I could with the knowledge that I had at the time and with the products that I was approved to sell. Financial advisors are also just doing the best that they can. They too must pay their car payments, pay their mortgage or rent, and put food on the table to feed their family. So please don't blame this situation on your financial advisor. The solution is to learn about the investments that your advisor can't tell you about—especially the ones that can deliver you an early retirement and enable you to retire tax-free.

Today, I never make recommendations; I only teach risk vs reward.

As for my wife, Stella, and I, our long-term focus is clear: creating passive income streams that we can start collecting now.

We invest to create "family banks" for investing and borrowing to strengthen each Pillar, and we track and measure our results by asking one question: "How much passive income do we have now?"

We may speculate for higher returns when buying stocks using margin, or even purchase a leveraged ETF after a crash—when stocks may be considered "on sale"—but we primarily invest for long-term growth and income.

IGNORE THE TALKING HEADS

Have you heard the talking heads on TV or on the radio? They say things like, "There is more risk investing in an individual stock than investing in a more diversified low-cost index fund, so only buy index funds."

It is true—there is less risk in an index fund. But it is also true that the top seven stocks, often called the "Magnificent 7," account for 30% of the performance of the S&P 500. So how diversified is your portfolio, really?

And is your "diversification" preventing you from making unusually high returns, especially after a market downturn?

Here is an example of how I invested in the past when I saw an opportunity:

It was March of 2020, and the S&P 500 had dropped about 34%, before it rebounded. I felt it had hit a bottom, and I decided to jump in with a few thousand dollars to "test the waters." I had the option of buying an individual stock or buying an index fund such as SPY. I also had the option of buying a 3x leveraged ETF (exchange-traded fund) on the S&P 500, ticker "SPXL." (If you are not familiar with SPXL, we will cover "the Good, the Bad, and the Ugly" about it a little later.)

I chose to use the leveraged ETF, which was betting up 3x, to earn 300% of the performance of the S&P 500, which I knew could make me a very high return. And since SPXL is also based on the performance of the S&P 500, it was also "diversified." I knew that the S&P 500 would eventually recover, and so would SPXL.

I had also found an article on marketwatch.com, about a "Millennial that bet most of his savings on one of the market's riskiest plays—and he's about to cash in $1.5 million."

In the article, a 20-something-year-old trader with a law degree, who goes by the name "Throwaway" on Reddit, decided to invest $170,000 into leveraged ETFs in the spring of 2010, betting that the markets would eventually recover. He claims he bought $100,000 worth of Direxion Daily Financial Bull 3X shares (FAS) and $70,000 of Direxion Daily S&P 500 Bull 3X shares (SPXL).

Throwaway experienced some serious volatility over the next year, but fast-forward to 2019 when Throwaway's portfolio had grown to over $1.5 million. We don't know if Throwaway sold his portfolio, but with the next market crash, I wasn't going to miss another opportunity to make some big money.

Now, I'm not recommending that you invest in SPXL. But it's important to know that 3x ETFs exist, and you can always start small to test the waters. Who knows—you might spot an opportunity the next time the market crashes. Remember, it's not *if* the market will crash; it's *when*. And when it does, how will you react to it?

I also think you should set a goal to become a "sophisticated investor" so you can see the opportunities that your financial advisor may not be able to see (or may not be able to tell you about even if the advisor does see them, because the advisor is afraid of "selling away"). A sophisticated investor knows to invest in all Five Pillars and earn returns far greater than the average investor—while also combining multiple tax strategies in multiple asset classes.

The First Pillar of our Buy, Borrow Die strategy is purchasing stocks and ETFs. What I love about this Pillar is that anyone of any income can start with just $100 and can invest in multiple ETFs with different characteristics to match their goals and risk tolerance.

What is even more important is that we can also borrow from our stocks and/or ETFs to build and strengthen the other Four Pillars.

Never kill the cycle of buying and borrowing. And the (tax-free) possibilities are endless!

8

Stocks and ETFs

The Good, the Bad, and the Ugly

> **stock**
> /stäk/
>
> *noun*
>
> part of the ownership of a company that can be bought
> by members of the public

Okay, let's cover "the Good," "the Bad," and "the Ugly" when investing in different stocks and ETFs.

INDIVIDUAL STOCKS

The Good

When you buy a stock, you own a piece of the company, which can provide a sense of ownership and potentially voting rights on corporate decisions. You can also buy fractional shares using many apps on your smartphone (iPhone or Android, whichever flavor you prefer) or your computer, so you can start investing with just $50 and auto-invest another $50 a week, for example.

- **Potential for high returns.** Individual stocks can offer significant returns, especially if you invest in a company that experiences substantial growth or if you invest after a stock market crash. If you never sell them, you never "realize" the gains, so you never get hit with capital gains taxes. Think instead of "buying" and "borrowing"—to pay no taxes.
- **Dividends.** Many companies pay dividends, providing a steady income stream in addition to any capital gains. These dividends are taxed, but extra taxable income is better than no extra income, right?

The Bad

Stocks can experience very high volatility, subjecting investors to huge price swings, especially when "fear" is high.

- **Individual stock risk.** Investing in a single company exposes you to risks specific to that company, such as management issues or competition, and that risk is multiplied by the overall growth and contraction of the economy.
- **Research and monitoring.** Most books about investing in individual stocks suggest you do "extensive research" of a company before you invest. To save you some time, I suggest you begin your research by Googling "the top 10 stocks of the S&P 500."

The Ugly

- **Taxes!** If you decide to sell before one year, you will be taxed at regular income tax rates, which are generally considerably higher than the long-term capital gains taxes if you held the stocks for longer than a year.

TRADITIONAL ETFs AND MUTUAL FUNDS

The Good

- **Lower risk.** Traditional ETFs and mutual funds offer **diversification** by pooling investments in multiple assets, potentially reducing the risk associated with investing in a single stock.
- **Lower expenses.** ETFs generally have lower expense ratios compared with mutual funds, making them a cost-effective investment option.
- **Flexibility.** Like stocks, ETFs can be traded on exchanges throughout the day, providing liquidity and flexibility, as opposed to a mutual fund, which cannot be sold throughout the day.
- **Transparency.** ETFs disclose their holdings daily, allowing investors to know exactly what they own.

The Bad

Different ETFs are subject to market risk, and their value can fluctuate dramatically, especially with the more complex ETFs, which may have less diversification.

- **Expense ratios.** While generally lower than mutual funds, ETFs still have expense ratios that can eat into returns over time. Personally, I don't care about expense ratios; I only see risk vs reward. The expenses would be "very high" on SPXL vs the low expenses of an index fund, but I think making 300% greater return is worth the "higher" expenses, don't you?

The Ugly

- **Taxes!** If investing in ETFs or mutual funds in a tax-deferred retirement account, all your gains will be taxable at the highest rates when you retire.

COMPLEX ETFs

Now, I'm assuming that you may not be familiar with a strategy known as a "covered call," so let me give you the basics. According to Investopedia:

> The term covered call refers to a financial transaction in which the investor selling call options owns an equivalent amount of the underlying security. To execute this, an investor who holds a long position in an asset then writes (sells) call options on that same asset to generate an income stream. The investor's long position in the asset is the cover because it means the seller can deliver the shares if the buyer of the call option chooses to exercise.

Sounds simple, right?

Now, before I lose you, and before your eyes completely glaze over, don't worry—this book is not a book on how to build complex options trades. The good news is that with recent non-stop innovation in ETFs, it is finally possible to buy a covered call ETF, and the fund manager with do all the "work" for you.

COVERED CALL ETFs

The Good

- **Income.** Covered call ETFs generate additional income through premiums received from selling call options. Traditionally, income from stocks has been paid quarterly, but there are many covered call ETFs that now pay monthly income, or in some cases even weekly income!

  For example, I own SPYI, which targets a 1% monthly dividend and 12% annual dividend, and is tax-advantaged by using "1256 contracts," which allow 60% of the dividend to be paid as long-term capital gains.

  I love competition, and I try to stay unbiased, so there are also some similar competitors on the market that I should mention. For example, newly created in 2024, a tax-advantaged competitor of SPYI is XDTE.

- **Downside protection.** The premiums/dividends can provide some downside protection in declining markets, especially when reinvesting the monthly dividends to buy more shares "at a discount" if markets are declining.

The Bad

- **Limited upside.** By selling call options, covered call ETFs cap the potential upside gains.
- **Complexity.** Understanding options strategies can be complex for average investors, but again, the work of selling options is done for you.
- **Potential loss of NAV (net asset value).** In volatile markets, the NAV of covered call ETFs can decline, particularly if the value of the underlying stocks decreases significantly. Loss of NAV is sometimes called "NAV erosion," which can happen to some covered call ETFs.

  However, because I always reinvest all my dividends, this NAV erosion can be offset by reinvesting all the dividends—to buy more shares and continually grow the income.

The Ugly

- **Taxes!** The taxes on these dividends, even when reinvested, are typically fully taxable at income tax rates.

  And if you put a tax-advantaged ETF inside a tax-deferred retirement account, you've converted all your gains, and all your dividends, into regular income tax rates on the back end. Ouch! I'd only recommend this strategy to those who believe the government is running efficiently, using tax dollars wisely, and, because of that belief, are eager to pay more of their "fair share."

SYNTHETIC COVERED CALL ETFs

The Good

- **Income enhancement.** Like covered call ETFs, synthetic covered call ETFs aim to enhance income through options strategies. Since these are generally used on highly volatile stocks, the income can also be very high when selling the options.
- **Cost efficiency.** Synthetic strategies can be more cost-effective by avoiding actual stock ownership and the trading costs (and risks) of trying to do it yourself.

The Bad

Synthetic ETFs involve derivatives (in this case, selling and buying of options), which are an added layer of risk. They have only existed in an ETF format since late 2022, so do your own research to see the past results when you read this book.

- **Single stock risk.** These ETFs carry single stock risk, similar to owning the underlying stock. For example, if Amazon crashes, AMZY is likely to crash as well; the same goes for NVIDIA and NVDY. To help minimize this single stock risk, you might consider a synthetic covered call ETF like YMAG, which is a "fund of funds" holding seven different ETFs within it.

  Full disclosure: I own AMZY, YMAG, and NVDY, but as always, please do your own research and due diligence at the time you read this book.

- **Complexity and transparency.** These ETFs can be less transparent and more difficult to understand due to their reliance on derivatives.
- **NAV erosion.** Because some of these ETFs also experience loss of NAV, receiving a "30% annual dividend," for example, doesn't necessarily mean your account will grow by 30%. Before deciding to buy a synthetic covered call, look at the "total return," and compare it with the performance of the underlying stock. If a fund loses too much NAV, look for an opportunity to sell it at the end of the year to benefit from tax-loss harvesting.

As part of a mix of other ETFs, these funds can supercharge the growth when **reinvesting all the dividends**.

Personally, I'll never take a dividend . . . I just keep reinvesting and buying more shares. If I ever need to access some cash, I'll just press the Borrow button and take a margin loan. To me, it's like "building a money machine."

The Ugly

- **Taxes!** These dividends—even when reinvested—are fully taxable at income tax rates.

LEVERAGED ETFs

The Good

- **Amplified returns.** Leveraged ETFs aim to deliver multiples (generally 1.5x to 3x) of the performance of the underlying index, offering the potential for high returns.

- **Short-term trading.** These ETFs can be suitable for short-term trading strategies and taking advantage of market movements. Because of the leveraged nature of them, you can bet up 300% on an index, or down 300%, using an inverse leveraged ETF.

The Bad

- **Amplified returns.** With leveraged ETFs you can bet both up and down and earn amplified gains or losses of the underlying index or security. If you buy the wrong one and the market moves in the opposite direction, you can find yourself in a bit of trouble. As a sophisticated investor, I love these ETFs, but I generally only use them after the market has crashed.
- **High risk and volatility.** Leveraged ETFs are highly volatile and can lead to substantial losses.
- **Decay over time, aka "NAV erosion."** The compounding effect of the daily reset of trading daily options, futures, and "swaps" can erode the NAV over time.

The Ugly

- **Taxes!** If you buy a leveraged ETF and sell it before one year, this will be taxed as ordinary income. If you hold it for more than a year, it can be taxed as long-term capital gains, but you also add the risk of experiencing a 300% loss if it moves in the opposite direction.

START OFF WITH BABY STEPS

In the end, it's up to you to commit your time, money, and energy to increasing your financial IQ. By learning the advanced strategies in this book, you'll be equipped to decide which ETFs align with your risk tolerance and what fits best in your Perfect Portfolio.

Over the past 25 years, I've devoted myself to finding the best ways to build wealth and minimize taxes, and this book is a collection of those discoveries. The good news? You don't need to become an options trader like I did. You can start small—invest just $100 in stocks or ETFs that handle the options trading for you.

Many of our students have opened accounts with platforms like Robinhood or M1 (with low-interest margin rates), starting with just a small amount spread across different ETFs to watch how they perform.

INFLATION AND OTHER RISKS

It is also vitally important to realize that the investment landscape has dramatically changed, especially since COVID, when the government decided that shutting down the economy and printing trillions was the best for us all. The famous words of Ronald Reagan come to mind: "I think you all know that I've always felt the nine most terrifying words in the English language are: *I'm from the Government, and I'm here to help.*" My immediate response is, "Thank you, but we don't need any more of your 'help.'"

The US government is on the fast track to bankruptcy, accumulating over $5.2 billion of debt each day. Unless there are massive changes, we will be $50 trillion in debt within the next decade, and to make things worse, the US dollar's dominance (thanks especially to the "petrodollar," an agreement from the 1970s between oil-producing countries to price and trade oil almost exclusively in US dollars) around the world is no more, with Brazil, Russia, India, China, and Saudi Arabia (and others) no longer using the US dollar to trade oil.

So, what is better? Stocks, ETFs, or mutual funds? The answer can be "all of them," "some of them," or "none of them." It depends on several factors, including what the economy is doing, and how you perceive risk vs reward, while also factoring in taxes and inflation.

Here are a few tax and inflation fighting tips:

- After a stock market crash, you may be better off selling your index funds (to realize the losses) and investing in individual stocks for a potentially higher return. It may be a good "risk vs reward" while also reducing your taxes. But once again, you are building your Perfect Portfolio, and your portfolio must be customized to your risk tolerance, your level of financial IQ, your tax bracket, and other factors.
- Rather than invest in an index fund in your retirement account, you may choose to invest in an index fund in your "taxable" brokerage account. If you never sell it, it appreciates tax-free, and you can borrow from the account secured by your ETFs.

- You may decide to invest in a blended account with many types of ETFs, including a portion in an index fund, a portion in a covered call ETF, or a portion in a synthetic covered call ETF (for example) while also buying and holding (forever) some individual stocks.
- The key is to understand how to reduce your tax bill and how to best strategically combine multiple strategies to do so.

JUST DO IT!

I believe you have the best opportunities ever with the rise of "free" trading apps like M1 Finance and Robinhood. I personally use M1 Finance to build custom hybrid portfolios, and I use Robinhood for stock and leveraged ETF speculation.

If you want to diversify, just pick another stock or ETF and invest an extra $200 a month, for example. I also suggest switching to weekly buys, like $50 a week, to take advantage of shorter fluctuations of the market. It's a slight improvement over monthly investing, but I've found that making weekly purchases helps with the psychology of investing—you get to see those extra shares add up throughout the month.

DON'T PROCRASTINATE!

Remember, the money press is running every day. So to expect less inflation in the future with another "Inflation Reduction Act" (which itself printed approximately 350 BILLION more inflationary dollars) that would somehow actually reduce inflation is not realistic (see Figure 8.1). It reminds me of the Elf on the Shelf: The gifts will arrive but only for those who do what they are told. But in reality, the "gifts" have been put on your credit card, and they are sending you the bill.

FIGURE 8-1   The slow crush of inflation on the American taxpayer.

I know, I'm repetitive at times, but only when I feel a message needs to be repeated. After reading this book, I hope you also develop a similar gag reflex to the one I have when you hear the words "Invest in your 401(k) to save on taxes" and "Don't worry; we will put you in a diversified portfolio of mutual funds." After all, that gag reflex might just save you from swallowing something that isn't healthy for you.

FINANCIAL ADVISORS

Don't get me wrong—there are some great financial advisors out there—but I have found that they are few and far between. In my opinion, true financial advisors should be able to answer the following question: **"How can I retire early and pay no taxes?"**

If they can't give you the answer in 60 seconds, ask them to read this book.

To avoid "the Ugly," never sell your assets.

9

Buy More and Never Sell

Using Fear and Greed to Amplify Your Returns

> **fear**
> /fir/
> *noun*
> an unpleasant emotion caused by the belief that
> someone or something is dangerous, is likely to cause
> pain, or is a threat
>
> **greed**
> /grēd/
> *noun*
> intense and selfish desire for something, especially
> wealth, power, or food

Everyone's heard the expression, "Buy low, sell high." Although, in theory, it sounds simple, trying to time the market has proved to be a great way to "buy high and sell low," once fear and greed are factored into the equation. One key thing that a lot of people also overlook is that buying and selling is *not* the strategy the most affluent families throughout the world have used to build mega wealth and pass it down to their heirs.

Let me tell you a quick story of Mark "Pat" Munroe. Mark was an American banker in the small town of Quincy, Florida. During the Great Depression, when the Dow Jones Industrial Average had plummeted by 89%, Munroe's advice helped birth 67 new millionaires; and by the 1940s, he put Quincy on the map as the richest town per capita in the United States.

This story began during the Great Depression, starting with the stock market crash of 1929. Unemployment began to soar, businesses began closing their doors, and the future seemed bleak for millions. Yet amid this storm of chaos and fear, Pat Munroe saw an opportunity to buy more shares of Coca-Cola, and he began telling his friends and his clients to do the same. Even when the stock crashed another 50% due to a dispute with the sugar industry, Munroe advised his clients to buy more, and even arranged to give them loans **secured by their stock** (hmm, doesn't this sound familiar?) to buy more Coca-Cola shares.

Munroe was a firm believer in the enduring value of Coca-Cola and believed that its stock was recession-proof. Munroe noticed that even during the harshest times, people would still spend their last few dollars on a refreshing bottle of Coke. It was a small luxury that provided comfort after a harsh day.

Munroe's strategy was simple: Buy more, and never sell. This approach harnessed the power of compound growth by continually buying more shares, always reinvesting the dividends, and never selling. The value of those shares and the dividends they paid even helped the town's shareholders stay afloat during future economic crises long after the Great Depression.

Munroe's strategy is sound today, and furthermore, the strategy has significant tax advantages. By not selling the shares, his investors deferred capital gains taxes indefinitely. This allowed their wealth to compound, with very little taxes, and those families were able to pass on that wealth to their heirs. Munroe also advocated for additional borrowing, secured by their stocks to purchase other assets (in one prime example, a local farmer came to Munroe to borrow $2,000 for farm equipment, but Munroe talked the farmer into borrowing $4,000: $2,000 for the farm equipment and $2,000 for Coca-Cola stock to act as collateral), so he may just well be the innovator behind buying and then borrowing.

As I write this today, I can imagine the diverging paths of two "investors":

Investor A was "investing" by buying a bottle of Coca-Cola each day: "It was just 5 cents a day."
      Investor B skipped buying the bottle of Coke each day and instead brought his bag of nickels to Munroe to buy stock in Coca-Cola.

If you were one of the Quincy farmers that listened to Pat Munroe and bought a share of Coca-Cola stock during its IPO (initial public offering) for only $40, you'd find that after the growth of the company, and after the stock splits of Coca-Cola in 1935, 1960, 1965, 1977, 1986, 1990 and 2012, and by reinvesting all the dividends, **that $40 would be worth more than $25 million today**.

See, getting wealthy and **paying no taxes** can be simple and easy. It's a simple matter of:

- **Buy assets. Never sell them.**
- **Always buy more**, especially during down markets.
- As the assets appreciate, **take loans secured by each asset to buy more assets**.
- **Repeat the process** of taking loans secured by assets only to buy more assets, and once again, **never sell** any of them.

Then just die. The key part of this step is to only buy assets you can pass to your heirs tax-free due to a stepped-up basis under current tax codes. A step-up in basis is like getting a free upgrade when you inherit something; for example, when you inherit, say, a house or stocks/ETFs, the value is "stepped up" to what it's worth when the previous owner passed away, so you can avoid paying taxes on all those years it went up in value—pretty sweet, right? That way your heirs inherit the stocks and ETFs you bought, and they don't have to pay capital gains taxes for the growth over your lifetime!

See, it *is* that easy!

This strategy only works if you can take loans secured by each asset.

Remember to only buy assets that get a "step-up in basis" (no taxes!) when you die.

10

Buy, Borrow, Die

It Really Is for Everyday Americans

> **eve·ry·day**
> /ˈevrēˌdā/
> *adjective*
> ordinary, typical, or usual

Now that I introduced the Buy, Borrow, Die strategy to you, you are likely thinking, "That's great, Mark, but how can I do it? After all, I'm not wealthy (yet)."

The fact is that anyone can implement a Buy, Borrow, Die strategy and eventually pay no taxes. The first step is simple: Invest in a taxable brokerage account. When you have over $2,000 in your account, you can borrow against it using a margin loan. And voilà! You've now started the first steps in the cycle of buying and borrowing to build wealth and avoid paying taxes!

Now I didn't build the tax system, but one thing that is important to understand about it is that **borrowing is tax-free, and working hard is highly taxed!**

Another important thing to understand is that a margin loan is likely very different than any loan you've ever taken in the past:

- There is no application.
- There is no credit check.
- It does not report to your credit report.
- And there are no required payments on the loan.

I know, once again it sounds too good to be true.

I told you the story of how I first discovered the "Buy, Borrow, Die strategy while building The Perfect Portfolio course. You may recall, I was showing our students a simple strategy for buying and then borrowing to invest. At that time, we were comparing brokers to invest, including Robinhood, Interactive Brokers, Fidelity, Schwab, and several others, as well as a newer broker called M1 Finance. M1 stood out as an outlier since it had a feature I'd never seen before: it had a Borrow button!

Interest rates were at record lows, and at the time M1 was offering margin loans at just 2%. Borrowing at 2% was the closest thing I'd ever seen to "free money," especially when purchasing a covered call ETF with a 12% dividend. Purchasing those ETFs with margin loans meant it didn't require any work to earn it, and more importantly, the loan was 100% tax-free. Do the math—earning a 12% dividend and then borrowing at 2% to then reinvest and earn a 12% dividend seemed fascinating.

My first thought was, "I'm already borrowing to avoid taxes." I felt certain that we were on the right path. I then began pondering about how we could use low-interest margin loans to buy real estate and other assets. My mind was racing out of control . . . calculating all the ways we could use tax-free loans to invest—and even create tax deductions when investing with money that had never been taxed.

It was in July of that year that *Forbes* published, "How Ordinary Americans Can Also Buy, Borrow and Die Without Paying Taxes." I knew right then that I had finally found the holy grail for legally avoiding taxes! But seriously, where had it been hiding all these years?

How could I have worked as a financial advisor and investment advisor representative, been training financial advisors for over a decade, and written three books about investing, money, and tax avoidance, and yet I had never even heard the words "Buy, Borrow, Die" as a tax or investment strategy?

That article mentioned that Amazon founder, billionaire Jeff Bezos, had used the strategy to pay no taxes from 2016 to 2018. No surprise there. But then it asked: "So, how can you do it?" It then mentioned that "M1 Finance offers M1 Borrow, which allows you to tap into your investments at as little as 2%." I realized that, without even knowing what it was called, I had been using the strategy, but it was good to know I was leading our students down the right rabbit hole.

We then spent the next three years enrolling hundreds of students in a beta test for The Perfect Portfolio course. It was a course taught over eight weeks, two hours a week, over Zoom, and we were showing our students how we were buying stocks and ETFs, but we never planned to sell any of them. We would then borrow (which is tax-free) to purchase other assets, and then borrow again in the future (yup, still no taxes) to purchase more assets. I know, that is a lot of ways to PAY NO TAXES.

The secret to making this strategy powerful is simple: Borrow only to acquire assets, never liabilities. Every investment is designed to generate income that can be collected at any stage of life, no matter what our students' age or where they started.

We will take you on a deep dive into the Buy, Borrow, Die strategy, but if you want to get started with a baby step, you can open a taxable brokerage account by scanning the QR code below. (Remember, the gains are only taxable if you sell, and we're never going to sell!)

Scan this for your first baby step!

11

The Basics of Financial Alchemy

Press Buttons and Create Money!

> **cre·ate**
>
> /krē ˈ āt/
>
> *verb*
>
> bring (something) into existence

Remember when we talked about financial alchemy back in Chapter 6, with the story of Jane? Well, now we're going to get into the basics of that financial alchemy and how to use it to turn lead into gold. Well, we're not really turning lead into gold, but we ARE creating money by pressing buttons.

Creating money by pressing the Borrow button sounds fun, and it is!

When you decide to create money for the first time by borrowing using a margin loan, it is important to ask yourself three questions:

Q: "Did I have to work for the money?"
A: No, you didn't.

Q: "Did I have to pay taxes on the money?"
A: No, you didn't.

Q: "Did I have to battle inflation while earning the money?"
A: No, you didn't.

To ask these questions will help you fully realize all the benefits, which you can then weigh against the risks. If the benefits outweigh the risks, then it's a good risk-reward ratio.

Let's assume, like Jane, you had invested $52,000 in your brokerage account, you were growing it tax-free, and you decided to pay off $22,000 of high-interest credit card debt with a margin loan. What is the risk-reward ratio?

- The obvious benefit is that you would be free of that predatory credit card debt that was robbing you of about $460 a month (a $950 payment with about half going to interest).
- The not-so-obvious benefit is that when you used a margin loan to pay off the debt, you didn't have to pay it down with after-tax dollars. You likely would have had to earn $640, pay your taxes ($179.20 assuming a 28% tax bracket), and then pay the $460 each month.
- Finally, paying off high-interest debt at 24–28% with a margin loan at 6.25% is an absolute no-brainer.

It is true that overborrowing using a margin loan can cause a "margin call" if the market begins to decline, but that is also for you to decide the risk vs reward. If you diverted the $950 per month you had been paying toward the credit cards into your brokerage account instead and used it to buy more shares, that reduces your chance of a margin call, and the account continues to grow and compound without taxes.

IS MARGIN INTEREST TAX-DEDUCTIBLE?

Margin interest, which is the interest paid on borrowed funds used to purchase investments, can be tax-deductible for the average American under certain conditions. However, there are specific rules and limitations to consider:

Investment Interest Expense Deduction

Margin interest is considered an "investment interest expense," which *may* be deductible on Schedule A of your tax return as an itemized deduction.

Keep in mind, the deduction is limited to your net investment income for the year, which generally includes interest, dividends, and certain capital gains. If your margin interest expense exceeds your net investment income, you can carry the excess forward to future years.

But to deduct margin interest, you will need to itemize your specific deductions on your return. This means that if your total itemized deductions, including margin interest, don't exceed the standard deduction, you won't benefit from deducting margin interest.

Limitations and Restrictions

Margin interest is only deductible if the borrowed funds were used to purchase taxable investments. If the borrowed money is used for personal purposes or to purchase tax-exempt securities (like municipal bonds), the interest is not deductible. (Gosh, it's almost like they want to incentivize you to buy things they can tax you on in the future. . . .)

There are also additional limitations based on your income level and other factors:

- **Not deductible for retirement accounts.** Margin interest incurred for funds borrowed to invest in tax-advantaged (or more accurately described "tax-deferred") accounts like IRAs or 401(k)s is not tax-deductible. So you can't borrow and create tax-free money and create a tax deduction by investing in a retirement account *using margin interest.*

  That is fine with me, as investing in a retirement account is just "kicking the can down the road" when it comes to taxes. Don't forget, you can't take a loan secured by **any** type of retirement account, and that is a deal killer for me—as it would kill the cycle of buying and borrowing.

- **Alternative minimum tax (AMT).** If you are a higher earner and are subject to the alternative minimum tax, the deductibility of margin interest may be affected, so see your CPA. If this applies to you, there are plenty of other ways to buy and borrow, and you will need a highly skilled CPA who also understands and uses the Buy, Borrow, Die strategy.

So the good news is that even ordinary Americans can deduct margin interest, but you must itemize your deductions and have sufficient net investment and/or dividend income to offset the interest expense.

With the standard deduction being relatively high after recent tax reforms, fewer people itemize their deductions, making it less likely for the average person to benefit. But when you embrace a life of buying and borrowing to invest, and you never plan to pay back the loans, the margin interest can add up and is an important expense to keep track of.

LAZY MONEY, DEAD MONEY, AND THE POWER OF SMART DEBT

According to an article in the *Wall Street Journal*, "Americans lost $603 billion by sticking with big banks." Their "lazy money" was sitting idle in the megabanks earning them an average return of 0.01–0.15%, when it could have been working hard for them in other places. It is important to remember that when your lazy money is not working for you, it is working hard for someone else, in this case a megabank—which can invest it and even lend it back to other customers at 24%+ interest.

Imagine how wealthy you could become borrowing money and paying just 0.01% to your "investors," while lending it out at 24% interest. Getting wealthy would be simple. You would take a $1 million loan (which is not taxed) and would be paying $100 a year in interest—while collecting $240,000 a year in interest/profit. Sounds great, right?

Now I'm very aware that we are not able to take a $1 million loan at 0.01% and invest it at 24%, but that isn't the point. The point is that not all debt is "bad." Debt is tax-free and *can* be a powerful tool for building wealth **with money that has not been taxed**. Your bank is doing it—so are the wealthy—and you can do it too.

It is always important to keep your money working for you, and this includes your short-term savings. For example, M1 Finance now offers an FDIC-insured savings account that currently pays 4.5%, whereas your megabank may only be paying you 0.01%. That may be an opportunity to earn a 45,000% greater rate of return on your money.

And don't worry—M1 High-Yield Cash Accounts are FDIC-insured up to $3.75 million, when your megabank is only insuring your savings up to $250,000.

At the time you are reading this, M1 may be paying a higher or lower rate, but either way it will be a much higher rate than the average return paid by the banks.

And when the Federal Reserve drops the rates, this is good news too, as it will also drop the rates we are paying when borrowing on margin. So when your savings rate drops, you can borrow at a lower rate for investing. It is a "win-win" scenario but only for the investors who borrow to invest.

It is "lose-lose" for all those who are just saving in their megabank accounts.

WHAT RISKS ARE YOU TAKING NOW?

There are always risks! If anyone tells you that something is "risk-free," they're not telling you the truth. I look at the savings accounts (at the megabanks) as very high risk. Seriously, go look at the rate on your savings account. Chances are you're probably earning less than 1%. If inflation is 4% (and currently it's a LOT higher than that), you're guaranteed to lose. "Guaranteed to lose" is very high risk!

If you defer taxes in a 401(k) or IRA and the government decides it needs to raise more money during your retirement, a larger portion of your retirement suddenly becomes the government's piggy bank. I also consider that a very high risk.

And what about Average Joe? Would Joe also be taking a high risk when borrowing $50,000 to buy more Amazon and Alphabet (Google) shares using a margin loan from a $6 million brokerage account? Not really. Even if Joe was borrowing another $2,000 a month on margin to buy more shares, it is a very low risk. When Joe is avoiding working hard, paying taxes, and fighting inflation to purchase his additional shares on margin, it is an acceptable risk vs reward.

What others see as high risk, I see as low risk; and what others see as low risk, I see as high risk. It is all relative to the perceived risk vs reward, which can change very quickly as you raise your financial IQ.

I'll assume that the question in your mind right now is, "This all sounds great, Mark, but when do I pay back all the debt?"

The answer is simple. You never pay it back. It gets paid off when you die. (Don't worry—we'll go over that too.)

To me, "Pay back your debt" translates to "PAY MORE TAXES."

You can save, invest, and borrow at M1 Finance. (So, what do you need a bank for?)

12

IRA

It IS a Retirement Account!

> **re·tire·ment**
>
> /rə ' tī(ə)rm(ə)nt/
>
> *noun*
>
> the action or fact of leaving one's job and ceasing to work

Gather around, boys and girls. It's time for a little history lesson.

Retirement planning changed in 1978 when Congress decided to alter the tax code. What followed was the creation of the 401(k) on January 1, 1980. You see, at the time taxes were considerably higher than they are now (the top federal tax rate in 1979 being over 70%), so it was originally created as a way for highly compensated executives to defer compensation from bonuses or stock options. It was never created to be a primary source of income for Americans; and even the father of the 401(k), Ted Banna, was soon critical of the plan, which according to him, "helped open the door for Wall Street to make even more money than they were already making." As of December 31, 2023, 401(k) plans held $7.4 trillion across more than 710,000 individual plans. Yup, that adds up to a lot of fees.

For many Americans, a 401(k) is better than not saving at all. One major benefit of a 401(k) for many folks is the forced savings toward the future. Since many Americans are addicted to spending, a 401(k) can be a good option since it forces you into saving *something* toward the future.

But what about those folks that are disciplined at saving? They've been told that "a retirement account is going to help reduce your tax bill." Does it really reduce taxes?

Let's review the facts about tax-deferred retirement plans and see if they do save you money, and if **you** can retire on them.

Let me introduce you to James, another student enrolled in The Perfect Portfolio course. James was married, had three kids, and worked at a large tech company in Washington State. James told me that he had followed the traditional path of going to school, getting good grades, and eventually graduating with a degree from Virginia Tech, a prestigious university. James let me know that he didn't come from money, and in fact he didn't get his high-paying job right out of school.

James explained: "I had been working at Starbucks, and there was a customer that came into Starbucks each day, and I'd built some rapport with him. As he frequented Starbucks for his daily Grande Skinny Latte, I began asking him what he did, and he let me know he owned a growing technology company. So I asked him to hire me. He told me no, but each day he arrived for his latte, I kept asking, 'Hire me for anything. I'll even come work for free for a bit if you just give me a shot.' He eventually gave in and started me at $40k a year. I outworked everybody, and soon my salary jumped from $40k to $80k as I began developing my skills in the technology arena. A few years later, I got a job offer at one the largest technology companies in the world, which also included a huge salary, which came in handy with a few more mouths to feed in the household. I reached out to you as my tax bill also had grown to over six figures a year."

James began asking me about the Buy, Borrow, Die strategy. "And what should I do with my 401(k)?" he asked.

I gave James a quick history of the 401(k) and other retirement plans, and it was a bit of an eye-opener for him.

James knew that 401(k) plans were just deferring taxes, but he had not calculated what would also happen after 20+ years of growth that would also be taxed as regular income during his retirement.

"And the distributions from your 401(k)/IRA can also cause taxation of your social security payments," I commented.

I continued: "As I wrote about in *Top 10 Ways to Avoid Taxes*, social security payments during retirement were meant to be tax-free, but in 1983 the government changed the rules to tax up to 50% of social security payments if your individual income is over $25,000, and for married couples if it's over $32,000. They changed the rules again in 1993 to tax up to 85% of your social security payments if your individual income is over $32,000, and for married couples earning over $44,000."

James looked a bit troubled. "Isn't that double taxation?" he asked.

"Yes, it is," I replied, "but because you are funding the social security trust fund with taxes, it is more like triple taxation."

James had been max-funding his 401(k) plan. He said, "That is what I was told is the best thing to do. Everyone is doing it." James was also clear, adding, "I don't want to work until I'm 60 or 65."

After a slight sigh, James told me he had about $500,000 in his 401(k) and he got a 6% match. With this information, I made some quick calculations.

"James," I said, "assuming you earn a 9% rate of return on your 401(k), and you only contributed the minimum to get the match, at age 60, you will have about $10.1 million in your retirement plan."

"Wow," he said, "that's a lot of money, and it is taxable, right?"

"Yes, it is," I told him, "and it's taxable at the highest tax rates when you take it out. Tax rates are going up in 2026 and will likely continue to rise in the future. And it sounds like a lot of money, but have you heard of the 4% rule?"

James sounded puzzled and replied, "No, I haven't."

"The 4% rule," I explained, "tells you how much you can take out of your retirement plan each year, so you won't run out of money during your retirement. It also been called the SAFEMAX rule."

I made a few more quick calculations and gave James the news: "Using the 4% rule, I've calculated that you will be able to take roughly $404,000 a year out of your 401(k) plan, but the 4% rule assumes you don't retire until age 65. And I've got some more bad news: The 4% rule was recently recalculated to 3.3%, so it will actually be about $333,000 a year."

James tilted his head and stared at me, "But what about the taxes? And what about inflation?"

"Good question," I answered. "Assuming an inflation rate of just 3% for the next 20 years, you will have approximately $184,000 a year for retirement, minus taxes at whatever the rates are then."

"But isn't inflation more that 3%?" James asked.

"Yes, it is more like 4–5% or more," I said, "but the government doesn't want to admit it, as it would be unpopular with the voters. So they just manipulate the numbers and recalculate the factors, and they remove food and energy to report a lower number. They need your vote, so they tell you a lower number—after they were the ones that voted to print more money—which created the inflation. I also talked about this in 2014 when I wrote *Rich Man, Poor Bank*. So, no, things haven't improved; in fact they have just gotten worse."

I continued, "So assuming an inflation rate of 5%, you will be able to collect about $125,000 a year, minus the taxes. And that should be just enough to trigger the taxes on your social security benefits. But don't worry about that! The social security trust fund is also on the fast track to bankruptcy, so you can avoid the 'triple taxation' since I don't believe you will collect a dime from social security. And unless something drastically changes, inflation over the next 30 years will reduce the value of $1 to just a dime."

James looked a little pissed. He said, "So why do they call it a retirement account?"

"It is a retirement account," I told him. "It is just not *your* retirement account. It will retire the executives on Wall Street, and perhaps your financial advisor will retire, and big government will also retire. It will fund their pensions and "free" health insurance with the taxes collected from your retirement plan.

See, they call them retirement plans because they do help a lot of people retire!"

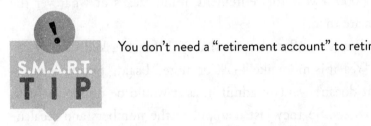

You don't need a "retirement account" to retire.

13

IRA

*It ISN'T a Retirement Account
(so Focus on Your Financial Independence)*

> **in·de·pend·ence**
>
> / ˌində ' pend(ə)ns/
>
> *noun*
>
> the state of being able to do things for yourself and
> make your own decisions, without help or influence from
> others

As you reflect on the previous chapter, consider the following: Since a retirement account won't ever retire YOU, why not delete the word "retirement" from your vocabulary? It is just a word made up by Wall Street (seriously, the Corning Company actually had a roundtable in 1951 to figure out how to sell the concept of "retirement" to the working class) to make you think that you need to work hard at a job for 30 or 40 years, pay your taxes, and one day you can "retire" with a "retirement account." That is simply not true.

Replace the word "retirement" with the words "financial independence," and ask, "If I focus on building passive income now, at what age can I become financially independent and work because I want to, and only on things that I enjoy?"

When your passive income exceeds your expenses, you can "retire" at any age.

Build passive income now!

14

Future-Proof Your Savings

Borrow to Fund the Tax Benefits of a Roth IRA

ben·e·fit

/ˈbenəfit/

noun

an advantage or profit gained from something

I can almost hear you asking, "But Mark, didn't you just say IRAs only help other people retire? Why would I want one?" Well, the key difference lies in how a Roth IRA works. Unlike traditional IRAs, the Roth IRA—named after Senator William Roth—was created in 1997 through the Taxpayer Relief Act. It offers a unique advantage, especially when it comes to how your contributions and withdrawals are taxed.

Here are the basics:

Roth IRAs are funded with after-tax money, meaning contributions are made from income that you've already paid taxes on. This crucial difference allows for tax-free growth and tax-free withdrawals in retirement. One of the downsides, however, is that there are income restrictions to consider. For 2024, individuals with a modified adjusted gross income (MAGI) up to $146,000 (or $230,000 for married couples filing jointly) can contribute the maximum amount. Contributions phase out at higher income levels, completely phasing out at $161,000 for single filers and $240,000 for joint filers, so Roth IRAs can be especially effective for folks who are earlier in their careers and aren't close to hitting those income limits (yet!).

CONTRIBUTION LIMITS

As of 2024 (and unchanged for 2025), the maximum contribution limit for a Roth IRA is $7,000 per year for individuals under age 50. Those aged 50 and above can contribute an additional $1,000 as a catch-up contribution (to literally allow you to catch up to where you'd be if you'd started younger), bringing the total allowed to $8,000 annually. These limits are subject to periodic adjustments for inflation, so it's essential that you stay updated on current thresholds.

WITHDRAWAL RULES AND EARLY ACCESS

One of the standout features of a Roth IRA, especially in comparison to traditional IRAs, is its flexibility in regard to withdrawals. Contributions can be withdrawn at any time without penalties or taxes, as these are after-tax contributions. However, to benefit from tax-free earnings, the account must be held for at least five years, and the account holder must be at least 59½ years old.

EARLY WITHDRAWAL EXCEPTIONS

Although Roth IRAs are designed for retirement, there are certain circumstances under which early withdrawals of both contributions and earnings are allowed without incurring penalties. These exceptions include:

- **First-time home purchase.** Up to $10,000 of earnings can be withdrawn penalty-free for a first-time home purchase.
- **Qualified education expenses.** Withdrawals for qualified higher education expenses are penalty-free, though taxes on earnings can still apply, so make sure you check with your CPA or tax advisor first.
- **Birth or adoption.** Up to $5,000 can be withdrawn penalty-free within a year of the birth or adoption of a child. Even with inflation, $5,000 can buy a lot of diapers.
- **Medical expenses.** Withdrawals for unreimbursed medical expenses exceeding 7.5% of your adjusted gross income are penalty-free.
- **Health insurance premiums.** If you are unemployed, you can withdraw funds to pay for health insurance premiums without penalties.

The Roth IRA offers an incredible mix of tax-free growth and tax-free withdrawals, making it a great choice for anyone who doesn't need access to their funds before turning 59 ½. While there are income restrictions and contribution limits to keep in mind, the ability to access contributions at any time— and even certain earnings under specific conditions—gives it a real edge. By understanding these rules, you can take full advantage of a Roth IRA to secure a more tax-efficient retirement. If you're looking for supplemental tax-free retirement income, especially after age 59 ½, a Roth IRA can be a powerful tool.

If you are one of our younger readers and are looking to retire early, I'll make the comparison between a Roth IRA and a "taxable" brokerage account, and you can decide which is best for you:

- A Roth IRA is funded with after-tax money, and so is a brokerage account.
- A Roth IRA grows tax-free, and so does a brokerage account.
- Dividends in a Roth IRA are tax-free, while dividends in a brokerage account are taxed.
- A Roth *can't* be fully accessed tax-free at any age, but a brokerage account can.
- You can fund *any* amount into a brokerage account, but Roth IRA contributions are limited annually.
- You *can't* take loans secured by a Roth IRA, but you can take tax-free margin loans secured by your brokerage account—giving you access to tax-free cash at any age, all while keeping your investments growing.

Here's an even smarter strategy if you want to enjoy the best of both worlds: Fund your brokerage account, and then consider using a margin loan to fund your Roth IRA. You can have the best features of both, and since you never paid taxes on the loan, your Roth IRA will have been funded with money that has never been taxed, it grows tax-free, you can take tax-free retirement income, . . . and yes, and you can die tax-free with both!

Yes, this is another strategy to **PAY ZERO TAXES!**

A Roth IRA lets you pass money to heirs tax-free, while brokerage assets can transfer tax-free thanks to a step-up in basis.

15

Shielding Your Wealth

Avoid Future Tax Hikes with a Backdoor Roth IRA

> **shield**
> /SHēld/
> *verb*
> protect (someone or something) from danger, risk, or
> unpleasant experience

The backdoor Roth IRA has been considered a strategy for HENRYs and high net worth individuals. "But Mark, my name isn't Henry," I can hear you protesting.

Don't worry—HENRY (in this case) isn't a name; it's an acronym. HENRY stands for "High Earner, Not Rich Yet," a description that applies to some of the students in our Perfect Portfolio course.

The backdoor Roth IRA is a strategic method that allows high-income earners to take advantage of the benefits of a Roth IRA, despite the income restrictions that would otherwise disqualify them. This loophole involves converting a traditional

IRA into a Roth IRA, providing a path to tax-free growth and withdrawals. Sounds pretty good, right?

WHY USE A BACKDOOR ROTH IRA?

Roth IRAs offer significant benefits, including tax-free growth and tax-free withdrawals in retirement. However, as we covered in the last chapter, direct contributions to a Roth IRA are restricted based on income. (As a reminder, for 2024, individuals with a modified adjusted gross income [MAGI] exceeding $153,000 [or $228,000 for married couples filing jointly] are not eligible to contribute directly to a Roth IRA.) The backdoor Roth IRA provides a legal work-around for these high earners.

HOW TO EXECUTE A BACKDOOR ROTH IRA

- **Contribute to a traditional IRA.** Begin by making a nondeductible contribution to a traditional IRA. (This is one of the few times I recommend making contributions to traditional IRAs.) For 2024, the maximum contribution is $6,500, or $7,500 if you are 50 or older.
- **Convert your IRA to a Roth IRA.** Once the contribution is made, convert the traditional IRA to a Roth IRA. This process involves transferring the funds from the traditional IRA to the Roth IRA. The timing of the conversion can vary, but many opt to do it shortly after the initial contribution to minimize any taxable gains.
- **Pay taxes on the converted amount.** Since the contribution to the traditional IRA was nondeductible,

only the earnings on the contribution are subject to taxes during the conversion. If there were no gains, the conversion is tax-free. However, if there were earnings, those will be taxed as ordinary income during the conversion.

CONSIDERATIONS AND POTENTIAL PITFALLS

While the backdoor Roth IRA strategy is straightforward, there are several important considerations to keep in mind:

- **The "pro-rata rule."** If you have other traditional, SEP, or SIMPLE IRAs, the IRS requires you to calculate the tax liability on the conversion using a pro-rata rule. This means that if you have pre-tax funds in any other IRA accounts, the conversion will not be entirely tax-free. The taxable amount is determined based on the ratio of after-tax contributions to the total balance of all your IRAs, so make sure you consult with your CPA and/or tax attorney.
- **How about business owners?** Yes, you can contribute to a SEP IRA and then convert it to a Roth IRA, but once again, there are specific steps and considerations involved in this process.

Contributing to a SEP IRA and Converting to a Roth IRA

1. **Contribute to a SEP IRA.** A Simplified Employee Pension (SEP) IRA is a retirement plan that allows

employers to make contributions to their employees' retirement savings. If you are self-employed, you can contribute to your own SEP IRA. The contribution limits for a SEP IRA are higher than those for a traditional or Roth IRA, which can be advantageous.

For 2024, the contribution limit to a SEP IRA is the lesser of 25% of your compensation or $66,000.

2. **Convert a SEP IRA to a Roth IRA.** Once the contributions are made to the SEP IRA, you can convert these funds to a Roth IRA. Here's how the conversion process works:

   - **Open a Roth IRA.** If you don't already have a Roth IRA, you will need to open one.
   - **Execute the conversion.** Contact your IRA custodian to initiate the conversion. You will need to provide instructions to transfer funds from your SEP IRA to your Roth IRA.
   - **Pay taxes on the conversion.** When converting from a SEP IRA to a Roth IRA, you will owe taxes on the amount converted. This is because SEP IRA contributions are made with pre-tax dollars and converting to a Roth IRA (which uses after-tax dollars) triggers a taxable event. The amount converted will be added to your taxable income for the year and taxed at your ordinary income tax rate.

Converting a SEP IRA to a Roth IRA

The pro-rata rule applies to all IRA conversions, including SEP IRAs.

- **Timing of the conversion.** Plan the timing of your conversion carefully to manage your tax liability. Converting in a year when your income is lower can help reduce the tax impact.
- **Tax planning.** Because the conversion will increase your taxable income for the year, it's important to plan for the tax liability. Consult with a tax advisor to understand how the conversion will affect your overall tax situation.

BENEFITS OF CONVERTING A SEP IRA TO A ROTH IRA

- **Tax-free growth.** Once converted, the funds in the Roth IRA grow tax-free.
- **Tax-free withdrawals.** Withdrawals in retirement are tax-free, provided certain conditions are met (the account must be held for at least five years, and you must be 59½ years old or older).
- **No required minimum distributions (RMDs).** Unlike SEP IRAs, Roth IRAs are not subject to RMDs during the account holder's lifetime, providing more control over your retirement savings.
- **Estate planning.** Roth IRAs can be passed on to heirs tax-free, making them a valuable estate planning tool.

WHAT IF TAX LAWS CHANGE?

I've been watching the chatter for years about how the government was going to "tax the rich" and "kill" the backdoor Roth IRA.

On November 1, 2021, CNBC then reported: "Backdoor Roth, a tax strategy favored by the rich, survives in Democrats' latest plan." While screaming "tax the rich," it was scrapped in the "Build Back Better" plan.

One thing I've learned about the folks in Washington is this: They only vote to "kill" a strategy after they (and all their big money donors) have implemented it themselves.

Convert an IRA to a Roth IRA in a low-income year or after a market crash to minimize taxes.

16

SPY vs SPY vs SPY

One ETF, Three Outcomes

spy
/spī/
verb

to observe or search for something

Now that we've covered the tax-free benefits of Roth IRAs and the backdoor Roth IRA, can I have your permission to challenge your thinking? Let's dive into what the most renowned financial experts, like Dave Ramsey and Suze Orman, have to say about Roth IRAs. Then, we'll reveal a completely different approach you've likely never considered. By the end, you'll be equipped to decide whether Roth IRAs truly are the ultimate retirement strategy—or if there's a better path to achieving your financial goals.

First, let's hear what Dave Ramsey has to say about Roth IRAs:

[The Roth IRA] really is the rock star of retirement accounts! Roth IRAs are easy to set up, simple to maintain, and come with tax advantages that help you build wealth and boost your retirement savings over the long haul. (*https://www.ramseysolutions.com/ retirement/roth-ira-101*)

How about Suze Orman?

In my opinion, you should absolutely be putting every single cent into the Roth version of your retirement account." (*The Ultimate Retirement Guide for 50 Plus*)

According to Orman, the Roth accounts give tax benefits, where contributions grow tax-free, and withdrawals are also not taxed. This enhances the retirement fund relative to traditional taxed accounts.

Pretty solid advice from both Dave and Suze, right?

Now, let's see what Robert Kiyosaki says:

My gripe with SEPs, IRAs, 401(k)s and RRSPs [Canadian retirement accounts] is that the financial institutions and the government push them so hard that people think they are the ONLY alternative. There are many other ways to save taxes that are much better for many people. (*https://www.richdad.com/ seps-iras-401ks-and-rrsps*)

Robert's view is more strategic, isn't it? I agree with him on that point, and now I'm going to back it up with some math and a deep dive into the tax code. Are you ready?

THE SPY EXPERIMENT

Let's compare three investors who all chose to invest in the same ETF, the S&P 500 index fund (SPY), at the start of 2008.

- Investor Ira buys $5,000 of SPY in his traditional IRA.
- Investor Dave (no relation to Dave Ramsey, of course) buys $5,000 of SPY in his Roth IRA.
- Investor Bob buys $5,000 of SPY in a taxable brokerage account.

All three invest $5,000 up front and add $416 a month to their portfolios. Fast-forward to the end of 2024, and Ira, Dave, and Bob each have around $248,000 in their accounts (based on historical SPY performance as of this writing).

Now let's compare their strategies—SPY vs. SPY vs. SPY—and break down the pros and cons of each approach, so you can decide which is best for you.

IRA'S TRADITIONAL IRA: A TAX TIME BOMB?

Let's take a look at Ira's IRA. You might not be surprised to hear that I'm crossing this off the list as a good option right away.

Here's why: Ira's IRA is just deferring income taxes to a later date. Yes, the account is growing—but so is Uncle Sam's share of it. Worse, when Ira starts withdrawing money, it could also trigger taxes on his Social Security benefits, turning tax-free

Social Security into taxable income. That's double (or even triple) taxation!

And there's another downside—IRAs are what I call "dead money" because you can't borrow against them. Plus, they don't pass to your heirs tax-free. Instead, the tax burden transfers to them.

So while the traditional IRA helps Ira save on taxes today, it creates a much bigger tax problem for tomorrow. That's why I prefer a Roth IRA over a traditional IRA for long-term tax avoidance.

DAVE'S ROTH IRA:
TAX-FREE ... BUT RESTRICTED

Now, let's move on to Dave, who also has roughly $248,000 in his Roth IRA. The beauty of this account is that Dave won't owe any taxes on this amount when he retires.

But what if Dave wants to retire early, say before age 59½? Unfortunately, he can't take out the full amount without penalties. However, he *can* withdraw his contributions (about $89,000) penalty-free at any time, which is a nice perk. Dave also has limited early withdrawal options, like using up to $10,000 for a first-time home purchase.

Still, until Dave turns 59½, most of his Roth IRA is locked away as "dead money" because he can't borrow against it.

BOB'S TAXABLE ACCOUNT:
FLEXIBILITY WITH SMART TAX STRATEGY

Now, let's look at Bob's taxable brokerage account. Bob also has $248,000, but unlike Ira or Dave, he can access his money anytime without penalties or restrictions.

The key is that Bob has read this book and doesn't plan to sell his assets, avoiding taxes triggered by selling shares. Instead, he uses margin loans to cover any expenses, including taxes on the dividends from SPY. By borrowing against his investments, Bob keeps his portfolio intact, allowing it to continue growing through compounding.

This reminds me of Charlie Munger, one of the greatest investors of all time. He famously said, **"The first rule of compounding is to never interrupt it unnecessarily."**

Bob takes this to heart. For example, he might borrow $89,000 as a down payment on real estate while keeping his $248,000 fully invested. Let's ask some key questions:

- Did Bob have to work for the $89,000? No, he didn't.
- Did Bob pay taxes on the $89,000? No, he didn't.
- Did Bob fight inflation over "X" number of years to earn $89,000? No, he didn't.

Instead, he created $89,000 at the press of a button, using it to grow his wealth further. Yes, he has debt, but the interest cost is small compared to the taxes he avoided. Plus, the interest can be tax-deductible.

Unlike Ira or Dave, Bob never has to touch his principal to access liquidity. When he passes away, his heirs benefit from a step-up in basis, potentially eliminating taxes on the appreciated value of his investments.

THE VERDICT: WHICH PATH SHOULD YOU TAKE?

So, what's the takeaway from this SPY vs. SPY vs. SPY comparison?

- Ira's Traditional IRA defers taxes today but creates a future tax problem.
- Dave's Roth IRA avoids taxes but has restrictions on early withdrawals.
- Bob's Taxable Account offers maximum flexibility and the ability to borrow while allowing investments to keep compounding.

OUR STRATEGY

I agree with Bob (and Charlie), and never disrupt the compounding of my assets. Here's the plan Stella and I follow:

1. Buy assets—stocks and ETFs, real estate, life insurance, cryptocurrency, and precious metals.
2. Never sell. Borrow against one asset to fund another, multiplying the compounding effect.
3. Pass everything tax-free to our heirs.

Does this sound better than the strategy you are currently using? If so, keep reading.

Don't just follow the talking heads—do your own research!

Make decisions that fit your strategy, not theirs.

17

Municipal Bonds

"Munis" for Tax-Free Money

> **bond**
>
> /bänd/
>
> *noun*
>
> an interest-bearing certificate of public or private indebtedness

In Chapter 3 of *Top 10 Ways to Avoid Taxes*, I wrote about the benefits of municipal bonds for tax avoidance. Munis can be a good investment for those that are in the highest tax bracket since the income received from investing in munis is exempt from federal taxes, which can be a savings of up to 37%. Yes, you read that right, no taxes.

But here's the scoop. In 2024, the current rate paid on a muni is only around 5%, but it is also a tax-free 5%. By comparison, it is also possible to earn 5% on an (FDIC-insured) savings account. Deduct 37% to pay Uncle Sam, you net just

3.15%. Obviously, earning 5% tax-free is a better choice when investing in a muni.

But it is important to remember, **when interest rates go up, bonds go down. And when rates go down, bonds go up.** The Fed raised rates in March of 2022 from 0.25% and held them through June of 2022. They continued to raise them until they peaked at 5.33% in April of 2024.

"So why do bonds go down when rates go up?" Good question.

Let's say, for example, you held a 10-year bond that paid a fixed rate of 3% (fixed for the next 10 years), and you wanted to sell it, but the Fed had raised interest rates by 5%; obviously, there would be no investors willing to buy your bond that paid just 3%. The value would drop dramatically. Yes, you would still be receiving the 3%, but the value of your bond would drop by about 40%. Ouch!

Municipal bonds can be a safe way to have some tax-free income, but it is also equally important to understand the effect of rising and falling rates, and you probably don't want to own bonds if you see rates will be rising. As I'm writing this, the Fed dropped interest rates in September 2024, and they may drop them again before the end of the year. It may be a good time to own bonds, but I feel that the dropping rates will once again "stimulate" the economy, and what will follow is higher inflation, which will erode the 5% return.

Personally, I don't invest in munis, as 5% is simply too poor a return when you also deduct for inflation, and there are strategies in this book that are far more effective for earning higher returns while also PAYING NO TAXES.

This is a tax book for "everyday Americans," so discussing strategies that are only effective for the wealthy is not my focus. I'd rather teach you strategies that anyone can use to end up with similar results, just like Average Joe.

"5% is a good return . . ."
Once again, it is like the blind leading the blind.

18

Minimizing Your Tax Bill

Strategies for Reducing Capital Gains Taxes

cap·i·tal gain

/ ˌkapədl ˈgān/

noun

a profit from the sale of property or an investment

Ever felt like taxes are designed to be confusing? You're not alone. The tax code is a constantly evolving, mind-numbing document spanning over 80,000 pages (when you factor in all the regulations, guidelines, and rulings). Even IRS employees struggle to explain it. Just when you think you've grasped a few key rules, chances are the IRS has updated them, a new administration has rewritten them, or they no longer apply to your situation.

Trying to understand taxes often feels like learning a new language—and that's because it is. It's the language of money, spoken fluently by bureaucrats, attorneys, and those who have mastered the skill of legally avoiding taxes.

I believe the reason they don't teach the language of money in school is because they need workers for the factories or for office cubicles, and they need millions of Americans to sign for new student loans (trapping those students in the cycle of debt). They also need to keep the masses ignorant, so they pay their taxes without question. The good news is that you don't need to take out a $100,000 student loan or spend years in school to learn to speak the language of money. You just need to raise your financial IQ a little bit every day. And as you read on, you can decide what is actual financial education and what is just bank propaganda to funnel wealth to big banks and big government.

My advice is simple: Don't worry about it! Just learn a bit each day. Treat this book as a guide and/or reference book and highlight the lessons as you learn them. And remember, once you learn the language, it's yours forever—no one can ever take it away from you!

Fortunately, many of the tax codes in this book have not changed for many years, and some have not changed for more than a decade. For example, the backdoor Roth IRA became possible because of the Tax Increase Prevention and Reconciliation Act of 2005, which became law in 2006. As I mentioned, this tax code has survived through to today, regardless of who has sat in the White House in the years since.

Another example is the Consolidated Appropriations Act of 2021, which introduced significant changes to tax code 7702. This tax code, often utilized by the wealthy, now allows them to shelter 100% more of their after-tax income into a life insurance policy, effectively doubling the amount compared to previous limits. This strategy provides triple tax protection: the cash value grows tax-free, tax-free distributions or loans can be accessed at any age (think, "buying" and "borrowing"), and upon death, the death benefit (plus the cash value) passes 100% tax-free to heirs. (Later in this book, we'll show how average Americans can also leverage this tax code.)

Finally, the American Rescue Plan Act of 2021 (aka the COVID-19 stimulus package) did rescue some Americans, but it also resulted in causing average prices in America to rise by 37.5% and gasoline prices to rise by over 115% as it "stimulated" the economy.

Now, let's get back to simplifying capital gains taxes and how it can help us all reduce our tax bill to ZERO.

Capital gains taxes are collected on the profit made after you sell an asset, such as stocks, ETFs, real estate, cryptocurrency, and other investments.

There are two types of capital gains taxes:

- **Short-term capital gains.** Taxes are collected when you sell an asset you held for one year or less. These gains are taxed as ordinary income taxes, which are the highest of all taxes and range from 10% to 37% federal taxes, plus the taxes that are collected by the state you live in. This could be as high as 54.1% if you happen to live in California, 51.8% if you live in Hawaii, or 51.55% if you live in New Jersey.
- **Long-term capital gains.** Taxes are collected when you sell an asset you've owned for more than one year. These are taxed at reduced rates, which are typically considerably lower than ordinary income tax rates. These are usually 0%, 15%, or 20%, based on your taxable income and filing status. Higher earners might also be subject to an additional 3.8% net investment income tax.

Exemptions and exclusions include:

- **Primary residence.** Up to $250,000 ($500,000 for married couples) of capital gains from the sale of your primary residence (the home you live in, in other words) can be excluded from taxes, provided you meet certain conditions (for example, if you lived in the home for at least two out of the previous five years).
- **Retirement accounts.** Gains in retirement accounts like IRAs and 401(k)s aren't taxed until you withdraw, but when you do, they're usually taxed as regular income, not at lower capital gains rates.

Rules for reporting and payment include:

- Capital gains must be reported on your tax return (usually on Schedule D and Form 8949.)
- Taxes are paid as part of your annual tax filing, but estimated taxes may be required for significant gains.

To summarize:

Capital gains taxes are only levied when you sell an asset. So if you don't sell it, you never pay taxes. Pretty simple, right?

And here's the real kicker: When you hold onto assets like stocks, ETFs, gold, crypto, or real estate, they get a step-up in basis when you die. That means your heirs can inherit them tax-free. No capital gains, no headaches—just wealth passed on without Uncle Sam taking a slice. Because at the end of the day, building wealth is one thing, but keeping it tax-free? That's the ultimate legacy.

 Never sell your assets, and teach your kids to do the same.

19

Turning Losses into Gains

How Tax-Loss Harvesting Can Save You Money

> **har·vest**
>
> /ˈhärvəst/
>
> verb
>
> collect or obtain (a resource) for future use

I covered tax-loss harvesting in *Top 10 Ways to Avoid Taxes*, but let's do a quick recap of how to avoid taxes in both up and down markets.

Tax-loss harvesting is the strategy of selling investments that have taken a loss (in other words, they've gone down in price or value), to offset capital gains and reduce your taxable income.

For example, if you sell an ETF at a $3,000 loss and have $3,000 in capital gains, the loss cancels out the gains. ZERO TAXES are due. The key is to "realize" the losses in a down market to reduce your tax bill, but also replace the ETF with a similar ETF and continue to grow your portfolio tax-free (see Figure 19-1). And remember, if you never sell, you will never "realize" the gains.

FIGURE 19-1   Walking the crops preparing for the next tax-loss harvest.

Here is a real-life example of a student who joined the course late in 2022 after the market had lost about 20%. She loved the idea of using the Buy, Borrow, Die strategy to invest in SPY, based on the performance of the S&P 500, but she wanted to know how to sell to realize the 20% loss without negatively affecting their long-term strategy of investing based on the S&P 500. To do so, she sold their shares of SPY and replaced them with a similar ETF, VOO, which is also based on the performance of the S&P 500. She realized the loss, but also bought an almost identical portfolio to replicate the same returns of the market when it recovered.

Tax-loss harvesting also works to offset dividend income, so realizing a $3,000 loss can also offset $3,000 of dividend income, giving you more money to invest instead of having to use it to pay taxes.

Pretty smart, eh?

Learn to reduce your tax bill by "realizing" the losses.

If you never sell, you will never "realize" the gains.

20

Borrow, Again

If You Can't Beat 'Em, Join 'Em

> **quan·ti·ta·tive eas·ing**
>
> / ˌkwän(t)ə ˌtādiv ˈēziNG/
>
> *noun*
>
> the introduction of new money into the money supply

I covered fractional reserve banking in Chapter 3, which will help you understand how the Federal Reserve prints money, which causes inflation, which silently, and progressively, steals your wealth. The more money that is printed, the more money "chases the same amounts of goods and services, causing prices to rise."

But that assumes that it is only the money that is **printed** that is causing inflation.

Here is the truth about inflation:

First, the money is printed at the Federal Reserve.

And yes, rather than call it "printing money," the folks in Washington make it sound so normal. It can even sound positive with phrases like "raising the debt ceiling," and "fiscal stimulus," and my personal favorite, "quantitative easing." WTF? What the fudge is "quantitative easing?"

Just imagine if they called it what it really is: "Print more money to pay *our* salaries and *our* health insurance—while funneling billions of your tax dollars to other countries," which may be a lot more accurate. But the problem (for the government) is that it's also a lot harder to sell to the voters.

Remember, when the government doesn't want to tax you (or at least, doesn't want to admit it's taxing you),the folks there simply sign another "stimulus" bill, which is really just a hidden tax, which, once again, steals from the poor and gives to the rich (and to the government).

Sorry, I went on another tax rant. I do that sometimes. But there was a point to all this, and to give you the rant but not offer a solution would simply be a waste of my rant.

So there is a simple solution, and it is incredibly important to understand if you want to stay afloat and ultimately secure your financial freedom.

The fact is we can't "print" money like the Fed, but as long as you can earn it, and as long as you also take your after-tax money and invest it, you too can "create more money" by borrowing against your assets. It's actually "new money," as debt. You create more of it every time you sign a mortgage, or every time you decide to take a (margin) loan secured by your stocks and ETFs.

The truth is, borrowing money is tax-free and can become your own personal "stimulus plan"—but only when you use it to buy assets that grow in value and generate income.

As those assets appreciate, why not add even more "stimulus" with another tax-free loan to acquire additional wealth-building assets? This is the core of the "Buy, Borrow, Die" strategy—mastered by the wealthiest families for generations.

They've been using it to build and protect their fortunes. Isn't it time your family did the same?

Inflation is printing money—beat it by "printing" your own through smart debt.

PART TWO

Real Estate

The Second Pillar of a
Buy, Borrow, Die Strategy

The Five Pillars

21

Unlocking Tax-Free Savings

The 2024 First-Time Homebuyers Tax Credit

> **tax cred·it**
>
> /ˈtaks ˌkredət/
>
> *noun*
>
> an amount of money that can be offset against a tax liability

When it was introduced in 2008, the first-time homebuyer credit provided up to $8,000 for eligible buyers. The goal was to encourage homeownership and stimulate the housing market during tough economic times (and 2008 definitely counted as "tough economic times").

The proposed First-Time Homebuyer Tax Credit Act of 2024 aims to provide a refundable tax credit of up to $15,000 for eligible first-time homebuyers, and has been drafted up but has not been signed into law (yet) as a finalized federal program. (I'll be crossing my fingers.)

When the credit finally becomes law, it will amount to a credit of 10% of the home's purchase price, with a cap at $15,000.

Here is some food for thought if you are eligible for the credit in the future:

Let's say you purchase a $400,000 home. If you bought that home with a $15,000 tax-free down payment from the government, and you signed a mortgage that creates another $385,000 (also tax-free money), you just bought a home with 100% tax-free OPM (remember, "OPM" means "other people's money"— and just to be clear about what it does *not* mean, see Figure 21-1).

FIGURE 21-1 This is definitely *not* what we mean when we talk about using other people's money to purchase assets.

You would now own a $400,000 home that can appreciate tax-free and that you never paid any taxes to earn.

You've now unlocked the power of OPM to create tax-free wealth using money that's never been taxed!

 100% OPM = 100% NO TAXES.

22

Leveraging OPM

The Tax-Efficient Path to Homeownership

> **lev·er·age**
>
> /ˈlev(ə)rij, ˈlēv(ə)rij/
>
> *noun*
>
> 1. use borrowed capital for (an investment), expecting the profits made to be greater than the interest payable
> 2. use (something) to maximum advantage

Billionaire investor John Paulson said, "If you don't own a home, buy one. If you own a home, buy another one. If you own two homes, buy a third. And lend your relatives the money to buy a home."

I agree with Paulson's advice, especially when you understand the $250,000/$500,000 home sale exemption, which we'll cover later in the following chapters. Think of investing as if you were playing chess: Your chess pieces are the different assets that you own, and you need each one to be able to move in different directions when you see an opportunity. I look at renting like only having 16 pawns lined up on the board. Even if you are a chess Grandmaster, you will eventually lose the game.

In Chapter 7 of *Top 10 Ways to Avoid Taxes*, I go over "Buy a Home Using 'OPM.'" This may be the most important chapter in that book, because I believe that homeownership is the first step to building wealth with no taxes. But it also highlights the importance of deciding whose advice you will follow—and the devastating consequences that result from following the wrong advice.

Let me give you an example. Let's use Investor A, Mr. Conservative, and Investor B, Mr. Risky.

It was 2019, and Mr. Conservative and Mr. Risky were both looking to buy a home, and they both wanted to live in the same neighborhood. They had both calculated that they can only afford to buy a home for around $300,000.

Mr. Conservative always had a dream of home-ownership. But first, he had to do his research and read all the books he could about investing and taxes, and, of course, learn about all "the advantages and disadvantages of homeownership."

Mr. Conservative began looking for properties and found his dream home at 1031 Scenic Drive, a two-bedroom, two-bathroom home in a newly developed community. Mr. Conservative was renting at the time and was paying $1,200 a month and felt concerned that he would be paying almost $1,800 a month for the new house once he added up principal, interest, taxes, and insurance. $1,800 just felt risky. He did his research, and after reading multiple books, he was convinced that he needed to wait: "I need to put a minimum of 20% down before I buy a home." Mr. Conservative put homeownership on the back burner, continued paying his rent, and was diligently saving.

Mr. Risky began looking for properties and found his dream home at 1033 Scenic Drive located right next door to where Mr. Conservative was looking to buy. Would Mr. Risky and Mr. Conservative become neighbors?

Mr. Risky was also renting at the time and was also paying $1,200 a month, but he also felt like renting was "burning his money" each month. It seemed risky, but he was known for that, and he decided to buy a home with just 3% down. He read about the dreaded "private mortgage insurance" (PMI) that he would have to pay because he "didn't put 20% down," but he had also calculated the tax benefits of owning vs renting. Mr. Risky moved into 1033 Scenic Drive and began enjoying the hiking trails throughout the neighborhood.

Mr. Conservative kept saving for a home, putting money into a savings account for a 20% down payment, expecting to buy a home in about 16 months.

What both Mr. Conservative and Mr. Risky could not possibly have factored into the equation was the coming pandemic, when the government turned the printing press on high and flooded the economy with trillions of dollars. Inflation quickly jumped to a 40-year high, and soon home prices began sky-rocketing. In an attempt to tame inflation, rates were rapidly increased, and a 3% mortgage became an 8% mortgage. No, Mr. Conservative did not end up being neighbors with Mr. Risky.

Now, I'm very aware that it was not possible for Mr. Conservative or Mr. Risky to predict the future, and especially to predict a pandemic. But predicting massive inflation after flooding trillions of dollars into the economy is easy. I took my "free money" and invested it and told my friends and clients to do the same.

I'll make another prediction right now, and if you are perhaps "Mr. Conservative," or "Mr. Risky," you can't say, "I didn't see it coming."

I'll predict that inflation will continue to get worse over the next 10 years, as the government must print more money to try and keep up the debt payments on the $36 trillion of debt it currently has. It will then print more again to pay the interest on the new debt payments, which requires the government to print more—and print even more again.

This will cause housing prices to double again in the next 10 years, especially in desirable, low-tax states.

The point of this chapter is not to try and predict the future, but to highlight all the flaws in the thinking of Mr. Conservative and how it caused him to pay more taxes and prevented him from buying a home when following the advice of the "talking heads" that don't understand how to use debt to build wealth and pay no taxes.

Let's look at the numbers and the tax savings, so you can decide the path that you take:

Mr. Conservative was focused on working hard, paying his taxes, and saving his after-tax money in his savings account. It can obviously take a very a long time to save 20%, or $60,000, after paying his taxes. Mr. Conservative was fighting both inflation and taxation and working harder each day to keep up.

Mr. Risky understood something that Mr. Conservative didn't. He understood that he could put just 3% down, yup, just $9,000 for a down payment; and by signing his 30-year mortgage, the additional $291,000 was created in a computer as debt, and debt is tax-free. Mr. Risky "created" $291,000 of debt and didn't have to work to earn a penny of it.

My hope is that 'Mr. Conservative' reads this book, buys a home, discovers the power of OPM, and invests in a second home to rent—before prices double again.

S.M.A.R.T. TIP

Put 3% down to buy a home.
Use debt for the rest, as debt is tax-free!

23

The Home Mortgage Deduction

Home Sweet Tax Break

de·duc·tion

/dəˈdəkSH(ə)n/

noun

reduces the amount of a taxpayer's income that's subject to tax, generally reducing the amount of tax the individual may have to pay

It is no secret that I love real estate. It has all the best tax benefits. The home mortgage interest deduction is a simple tax break that allows homeowners to deduct the interest paid on their home loans from their taxable income. This can be a powerful tax reduction tool—especially when you understand that taxes are "progressive," meaning that when you jump into a higher tax bracket, it cuts even deeper.

This mortgage deduction can result in significant tax savings and make homeownership even more affordable.

Let me give you an example, assuming a $400,000 mortgage at a 7% interest rate:

In this case, the mortgage principal and interest payment would be $2,662.21 a month.

The interest is $2,333.33 with just $327.88 going toward principal. This is where people freak out: "What, only $327.88 toward principal?! I'll send extra payments to pay it off quicker." This seems logical when you don't understand taxes. Paying extra principal means paying more in taxes as the deduction drops each time you pay down principal, resulting in higher taxes. And most importantly, while freaking out, they didn't factor in that the $400,000 that was borrowed to purchase the home was 100% tax-free.

To qualify for the mortgage interest deduction, it is important to know the current tax laws and verify they haven't changed from year to year. The good news is that many of the tax codes having to do with homeownership rarely change.

Here are the rules (current as of September 2024):

- The mortgage must be secured by your primary or secondary home.
- The interest is only deductible up to the first $750,000 ($375,000 if married filing separately) for loans taken out after December 15, 2017. For loans taken before this date, the limit is $1 million ($500,000 if married filing separately).

- The loan must be used to buy, build, or substantially improve your home.

This is valuable at tax time when you can deduct the interest paid on your mortgage, reducing your taxable income, which can place you in a lower tax bracket and decrease the amount of taxes you owe.

This is where the so-called financial "experts" tell you to put the biggest down payment on your home and make extra payments to reduce interest. Are they working for the IRS? Why would you throw more money at your mortgage just to PAY MORE TAXES?

Pay your January mortgage payment in December to boost your mortgage interest deduction for the current tax year.

24

The $250,000/$500,000 Home Sale Exemption

Tax-Free Home Sale Jackpot

> **ex·emp·tion**
> /igˈzem(p)SH(ə)n, egˈzem(p)SH(ə)n/
> *noun*
> the process of exempting a person from paying taxes on a specified amount of income for themselves and their dependents

I've got some simple advice for those who want to buy real estate: "Buy one to live in and one to rent."

I was just 19 years old when the $250,000/$500,000 home sale exemption was created under the Taxpayer Relief Act of 1997. The home sale exemption was designed to encourage homeownership by providing tax relief to those selling their primary residence. It was signed into law by Bill Clinton and became effective for home sales after May 6, 1997. This is another example of a tax law that has been around for more than 25 years, and yet very few people know how to use it to make millions and PAY NO TAXES.

I've used this exemption three times in the past 20 years to make hundreds of thousands of dollars completely tax-free. I first learned about the exemption back in 2005 when I sold my condo, netting $120,000 completely tax-free. I used it again in 2007 and 2014. The best part? You can use this strategy every two years!

Let me first give you the basics of how the $250,000/$500,000 homeowner exemption works:

- This exemption allows you to exclude up to $250,000 of capital gains from income if you are single, and up to $500,000 if you are married and file jointly.
- To qualify for the exemption, you need to live in the property as your primary residence for at least two out of the last five years before selling. Also, you can't have used the exemption on another property in the past two years. (It's important to note the specific wording: You "must live in the property as your primary residence for two of the last five years" before the sale.)

Now, imagine the possibilities if you have "one to live in and one to rent." You could buy your first home with just 3% down, live there for two years, then rent it out while purchasing a second property (again with just 3% down) as your new primary residence.

Fast-forward 15 years. You decide that you want to sell both properties and retire somewhere tropical. Here's how the math might work:

- You sell your primary residence which has appreciated by $500,000. Since you lived in it for two of the last five years before the sale, you can exclude the entire gain. Assuming you are married and filing jointly, that's **$500,000 completely tax-free!**
- You move into your rental property and live there for (another) two years before selling. Over the years, its value has appreciated by $400,000. Since you lived in the home as your primary residence for two of the last five years (a total of 4 years during your ownership), you can exclude $94,000 of the gain from taxes.
- However, the remaining $306,000 in gains would likely be subject to long-term capital gains taxes, typically around 20%. Depending on your income, state, and other factors, the tax could be approximately $61,200. Not bad, considering the gain. That means, after selling both properties, you could walk away with approximately **$840,000 tax-free!**

Keep in mind, this is an oversimplified example and doesn't include depreciation recapture (which we will cover in a later chapter) which could increase your tax bill when selling a rental property. Even so, the numbers are still impressive, especially considering your mortgage balances on both properties would likely be significantly reduced. This means even more cash in your pocket—perfect for enjoying piña coladas under a coconut tree.

Now, I did say you could "make millions and PAY NO TAXES," so why stop there? Why not have "one to live in and nine to rent"? It'll involve a lot of moving every two years, but the potential for wealth accumulation is huge.

Or . . . you could take that $840,000, invest it, never sell, and "live off the Borrow button." That way, you'll never have to work—or pay taxes—again. We'll explore that strategy later in the book!

   Be S.M.A.R.T.er than your financial advisors.

25

Depreciation on Rental Property

Tax-Free Income for Real Estate Investors!

> **de·pre·ci·a·tion**
>
> /də͵prēSHē'āSH(ə)n/
>
> *noun*
>
> a reduction in the value of an asset with the passage of
> time, due to wear and tear

I 've said it before, and I'll say it again—I simply love real estate! It offers powerful tax benefits, especially when you combine it with the strategy of buying and borrowing.

In Chapter 9 of *Top 10 Ways to Avoid Taxes*, I gave a simple definition of how depreciation can help generate tax-free income, but let's recap the basics and tie it into the Buy, Borrow, Die strategy.

Depreciation allows property owners to deduct the cost of their property over time, based on its wear and tear. This deduction can offset rental income, reduce taxable income, and, in many cases, result in tax-free income. Who wouldn't want tax-free income, right? After all, that's why you're reading this book!

Depreciation is like making money when things go down in value. Here's how it works: Your property can be increasing in value on paper, growing tax-free, but at the same time, you get to say it's going down in value—which reduces your taxes!

For example, imagine you purchase a rental property for $400,000, with $330,000 attributed to the building and $70,000 to the land. You can't depreciate land, but you can depreciate the building, which is worth $330,000.

Here are the numbers:

The building value is $330,000.

The depreciation period for residential property is 27.5 years.

Annual depreciation deduction: $330,000/27.5 = **$12,000**.

This is an oversimplified example, but assuming you collected $12,000 of rent after expenses that year, the depreciation would offset the rents, and the $12,000 would be tax-free.

Obviously, a $400,000 property should produce far more rent, so let's assume it generates $40,000 of rental income, but you also include the other common expenses of owning a rental property.

In this example, assume the following:

Mortgage: $15,000 total, of which $12,000 is interest

Property taxes: $4,000

Maintenance and management fees: $3,000

Insurance: $1,000

This means that you'll have $20,000 in tax deductions, even though you had cash payments of $23,000.

Now, let's calculate the taxable income by subtracting both the actual expenses and the depreciation deduction from the rental income:

Rental income: $40,000

Total annual tax deductible expenses (excluding depreciation): $20,000

Annual depreciation deduction: $12,000

Total tax deduction: $32,000

Income of $40,000 – $32,000 of expenses = $8,000 taxable income

Income of $40,000 – $23,000 of cash payments = $17,000 of positive cash flow (aka the amount you actually deposit in your bank account)

Thanks to depreciation, you're only taxed on $8,000, even though you pocketed $17,000. This means $9,000 of your cash flow is completely tax-free!

By utilizing depreciation, you significantly reduce the amount of taxable income from your rental property. In this example, instead of paying taxes on the full $40,000 of rental income, deductions and depreciation have shielded 80% of your gross rental income. Even better, you've deposited $17,000 in your bank account, while only being taxed on $8,000, giving you **untaxed cash flow of $9,000!**

This powerful tax strategy highlights the advantages of real estate investments and demonstrates how depreciation can significantly reduce taxable income. By reinvesting these savings, you can accelerate your wealth-building journey, using tax-free or reduced-tax income to acquire more assets and expand your portfolio. Depreciation is one of the most valuable tools available to real estate investors, and it becomes even more impactful when combined with **cost segregation**, **accelerated depreciation**, and **bonus depreciation**—all of which we will explore in the following chapters.

Maximize your depreciation and reinvest your tax savings into powerful tax-free assets to amplify your wealth!

26

Cost Segregation

Boosting Tax-Free Income for
Real Estate Investors

---

seg·re·ga·tion

/ˌsegrə'gāSH(ə)n/

noun

the separation for special treatment of items from a
larger group

As I dive into these advanced strategies for avoiding taxes while investing in real estate, I want to be up front—these strategies aren't "simple and easy to understand," which was my goal when writing this book.

But this chapter and the two that follow, when combined with buying and borrowing, are the key to "how the rich pay no taxes." The best part? Any ordinary American can do it too. The tax code doesn't discriminate—the same rules apply to everyone, no matter their income, race, background, or pedigree.

As with all my investments, whether time or money, I always measure the cost versus the benefit.

We start with this question: "What do I need to invest, and what will my family gain?"

Let's say it took you 100 hours reading this book and watching videos to better understand each of the strategies. You figure, "I could save at least $100,000 in taxes over the next five years by using these strategies." What's the cost vs benefit? Well, 100 hours of your time, divided by $100,000 in savings, equals $1,000 per hour for learning how to legally avoid taxes. Is that worth it?

I'm actually underselling the value when I say it's worth $1,000 an hour. Implementing these strategies in real estate could save you millions of dollars—and even help you pay no taxes on all forms of income, including your job and dividend income! I know it sounds too good to be true, but I promise, it's not.

Stella and I use multiple tax strategies simultaneously every year, and we estimate they'll save us at least $1 million in taxes over the next 10 years. If you follow our example, your 100 hours of learning could be worth $10,000 an hour for you and your family. How's that for cost versus benefit?

UNDERSTANDING COST SEGREGATION

Cost segregation is a powerful tax strategy that allows real estate investors to accelerate depreciation deductions, significantly reducing their taxable income and increasing their tax-free cash flow.

This technique involves breaking down a property into its individual components and pieces and depreciating them over shorter life-spans than the standard "27.5 years" for residential real estate or "39 years" for commercial properties. (The difference between commercial vs residential is that commercial real estate is considered four or more units, and one to four units are considered residential real estate.)

When you purchase a property, not all parts of it wear out at the same rate. For example, the carpeting, appliances, and landscaping may have a shorter useful life compared with the life of the building structure itself. Cost segregation identifies and reclassifies these shorter-lived components, allowing investors to depreciate them more quickly.

Think about it—would the carpeting last 27½ years? So why would it be depreciated at the same rate as the roof or the framing and drywall?

Under standard depreciation, a residential rental property is depreciated over 27.5 years, which means you can deduct approximately 3.64% of the building's value each year. With cost segregation, certain components can be depreciated over 5, 7, or 15 years, resulting in larger deductions in the early years of ownership. Again, this accelerating of the depreciation increases the tax-free cash flow from real estate.

The first step is a property analysis, or cost segregation report, completed by a specialist who analyzes the property and identifies components that qualify for shorter depreciation periods.

I recently used a DIY cost segregation firm to complete a cost seg report for a property we own in Tennessee, and we paid just $495 for the report.

Note that in a cost seg report, components such as the fixtures, plumbing, electrical systems, and landscaping can be reclassified from a 27.5-year schedule (or 39-year if commercial) to a 5-, 7-, or 15-year depreciation schedule. This is commonly known as "accelerated depreciation" and results in faster and larger depreciation deductions in the initial years.

Here is another simplified example:

Let's say you purchased a residential rental property for $500,000, with $400,000 allocated to the building and $100,000 to the land. Under standard depreciation, you would deduct approximately $14,545 per year ($400,000/27.5 years).

Now, imagine a cost segregation study reveals that $100,000 of the building's value can be reclassified into 5-year property. This means you can depreciate this $100,000 over 5 years instead of 27.5 years.

Cost segregation depreciation would be as follows:

5-year property: $100,000/5 = $20,000 per year vs the $14,545 without cost seg

Remaining 27.5-year property: $300,000/27.5 = $10,909 per year

Total annual depreciation for the first 5 years: $20,000 + $10,909 = $30,909

By using cost segregation, you can deduct $30,909 per year for the first five years, compared with just $14,545 with standard depreciation. That's an extra $16,364 in deductions each year for the first five years!

As I mentioned before, standard depreciation (aka "straight-line depreciation") allows you to say the property is "losing value" and reduce your taxes—even if the property is appreciating in value.

Accelerated depreciation takes these benefits to the next level in the first five to fifteen years, freeing up more tax-free money to reinvest in real estate and continue building your Buy, Borrow, Die strategy. But here's the catch: never sell. If you do, the benefits of accelerated depreciation can backfire because you'll have to "recapture" that depreciation, potentially undoing the tax savings you've worked so hard to achieve. On the other hand, if you hold onto the property until you pass away, it transfers to your heirs tax-free—and if they rent it out, they can start depreciating it all over again, creating even more tax-free income.

Anyone else want to create multi-generational income and wealth that's truly tax-free?

To fully leverage accelerated and bonus depreciation, invest in positive cash flow real estate.

27

Bonus Depreciation

*Supercharging Tax-Free Income
for Real Estate Investors*

> **bo·nus de·pre·ci·a·tion**
>
> /ˈbōnəs dəˌprēSHēˈāSH(ə)n/
>
> *noun*
>
> an additional first-year depreciation allowance
> that allows business taxpayers to deduct additional
> depreciation for the cost of qualifying business property,
> beyond normal depreciation allowances

I know what you're thinking now: "Mark, wow, there's sure a lot of ways to make my real estate income tax-free!" And you're right, there are. But just like those late-night infomercials, this is the point where I go, "But wait, there's more!" Now, we come to one of my favorite strategies for truly supercharging your tax-free income: BONUS DEPRECIATION.

Bonus depreciation is a powerful tool for real estate investors, letting you speed up the depreciation on certain property assets. This helps you reduce your taxable income faster and boost your cash flow.

This tax incentive was made even stronger by the Tax Cuts and Jobs Act (TCJA) of 2017, making it better than ever for real estate investors. In this chapter, we'll explore what bonus depreciation is, how it works, and how it can benefit real estate investors by providing even more tax-free income.

UNDERSTANDING BONUS DEPRECIATION

Bonus depreciation is like a tax gift for real estate investors—letting you instantly write off a huge chunk of the cost of eligible property the year it's put to use. Instead of slowly depreciating assets over time, bonus depreciation let's you say, "Why wait?" and take that deduction up front. Thanks to the Tax Cuts and Jobs Act, this deduction jumped to a whopping 100% for qualified properties acquired after September 27, 2017, and before January 1, 2023. Talk about a turbo boost!

KEY FEATURES OF BONUS DEPRECIATION

Here's the magic for real estate investors: You can accelerate both regular and bonus depreciation to score a hefty deduction in the first year. Imagine buying a commercial property and fast-forwarding 39 years' worth of depreciation all at once, creating what looks like huge "losses." But don't worry—you're not actually losing money! You're just using the depreciation to wipe out taxable income. It's like waving a wand and watching your tax bill disappear. In fact, some savvy investors have used this trick to pay zero taxes for multiple years. How's that for a win?

Now, accelerated and bonus depreciation doesn't just apply to real estate.

It can also apply to tangible property (in other words, things you can touch) with a recovery period of 20 years or less, such as machinery, equipment, and certain improvements to commercial property.

These deductions also apply to new and used property (so this doesn't just apply to newly built houses or commercial buildings). Under the TCJA, bonus depreciation applies to both new and used property, provided it is the first use of the property by the taxpayer (so it doesn't have to be new; it just has to be "new to you").

The good news is that this has meant massive tax savings (up to 100% of the value!) in the past, but the bad news is that the 100% bonus depreciation rate is scheduled to be slowly phased out after 2022, reducing by 20% each year until it is completely phased out by 2027. So depending on what year you purchased your real estate will determine the effectiveness of using accelerated and bonus depreciation to offset real estate income.

The phase-out schedule is as follows:

- 80% bonus depreciation for property placed in service in 2023
- 60% bonus depreciation for property placed in service in 2024
- 40% bonus depreciation for property placed in service in 2025
- 20% bonus depreciation for property placed in service in 2026
- 0% bonus depreciation for property placed in service in 2027 and beyond. (Insert sad noises here.)

Let's consider a simplified example to illustrate how bonus depreciation works and the additional tax savings it can provide.

Imagine you purchase a commercial property for $1 million. Of this amount, $800,000 is allocated to the building, and $200,000 is allocated to various tangible assets such as equipment, furniture, and fixtures, all of which qualify for bonus depreciation.

So how would your depreciation look if not using bonus depreciation?

You would receive a standard depreciation for the building (spread out over 39 years): $800,000/39 = $20,513 per year.

The standard depreciation for the tangible assets (spread out over 7 years) would be $200,000/7 = $28,571 per year.

So your total annual depreciation without bonus depreciation would be $20,513 + $28,571 = $49,084.

And how much could you save with bonus depreciation (if we assume we're doing these calculations in 2022)?

You could take an immediate deduction for the tangible assets, which is a deduction of $200,000 (100% of the cost) up front vs the $28,513 with straight-line depreciation.

The standard depreciation for the building is the same: $20,513 per year.

In the first year, the total depreciation deduction would be:

Bonus depreciation: $200,000 (immediate deduction)

Standard depreciation: $20,513 (building)

Total first-year depreciation: $200,000 + $20,513 = $220,513

By applying bonus depreciation, you can deduct $220,513 in the first year instead of $49,084. This final result is less taxable income, aka more tax-free income—to acquire more real estate.

As I write this today, bonus depreciation is a powerful tool for real estate investors, enabling them to accelerate depreciation deductions and reduce taxable income significantly. The enhancements brought by the TCJA, including the 100% deduction for qualified property and for used property, have made bonus depreciation even more effective. By utilizing bonus depreciation, investors can boost cash flow, reinvest tax savings, and amplify wealth growth through the compounding benefits of buying and depreciating real estate.

We don't know what the future will hold if the benefits of the TCJA will be extended, but this strategy can be most effective for any investors that bought a rental property prior to 2023. As of the time we're writing this, there is a benefit up until the end of 2027, but it is dramatically reduced.

Historically, tax rates almost always go up. Plan accordingly.

28

Business Ownership and Rental Income

Buy One to Live In and One to Rent

ren·tal prop·er·ty

/ˈren(t)l ˈpräpərdē/

noun

a real estate asset that is owned by an individual or entity
and is made available for lease or rent to tenants

I have the same advice for any new real estate investor regardless of whether the tax benefits of the TCJA are extended: "Buy one to live in and one to rent."

You don't need bonus depreciation to build wealth in real estate; you just need to build a foundation of one home to live in, and then set a goal to buy one home to rent, and repeat.

Even standard depreciation can help reduce your taxes, and you can still use accelerated depreciation to further reduce your tax bill. And when you own a rental property, you also now own a business, and with that you can discover the additional tax benefits of business ownership. Don't worry; we will cover those a little later in the book.

So if you already own a home and are thinking about buying a rental property, here are a few hacks to use OPM (other people's money) and take advantage of the benefits that come from both business ownership and rental income.

Let's say you bought your primary residence before 2023 and now want to invest in a rental property. Instead of buying a rental property, which usually requires a large down payment, here's what you can do: Rent out your current home and buy a new property to live in as your primary residence. Like we mentioned earlier in the book, since you're purchasing this as your main home, you can put down just 3%. That's right—only 3% of the purchase price comes from you, while 97% is OPM—borrowed money that's completely tax-free. It's like creating tax-free money to help you secure your dream home!

Now, your old home is officially your rental property—congratulations! You've also just started a business. Make sure you fully understand the tax codes we've discussed and partner with a CPA who truly knows how to navigate rental property ownership while leveraging multiple tax-avoidance strategies. If they give you a blank stare when you ask, "Can you explain how bonus depreciation helps save on taxes?" hand them a copy of this book and see if they'd be willing to read it.

However, if they read it and still come back with, "Just add more to your retirement account to save on taxes," well, it might be time to start shopping for a new "tax professional."

The great news is that because you bought your rental property when bonus depreciation was beginning to phase out, you would still be eligible to use accelerated depreciation, along with bonus depreciation, since you acquired the property before 2023.

I know you're thinking: "But what happens when bonus depreciation completely phases out?" Well, do you want some great news? There's no "phase-out" for buying stocks and ETFs, growing them tax-free, and borrowing from them tax-free for your next real estate down payment using OPM—which is also tax-free.

Bonus and accelerated depreciation from Trump's Tax Cuts and Jobs Act were game-changers. Stay tuned—new deductions could unlock fresh wealth-building opportunities!

29

Real Estate Professional Status

The "Secret Sauce" to Pay No Taxes

pro·fes·sion·al

/prə'feSH(ə)nəl/

noun

a person engaged in a specified activity as a main paid occupation rather than as a pastime

Every great recipe has that secret ingredient that's passed down through the generations, something that few folks know about, that makes it taste better. It's always something that when you learn about it, you think, "That's it? That's what makes it all work so well?" When it comes to using real estate to pay no taxes, real estate professional status (REPS) is what makes the secret sauce work. Without REP status, you still have the makings of something good, but REPS is what can make the mixture of all the other ingredients great.

While living in California over the past two decades, it was very common among married couples for one spouse to have a job and one spouse to be self-employed working in real estate. I didn't fully understand what tax codes they were using to potentially pay no taxes, partly because I was a financial advisor, so I thought it didn't apply to me. But if I had known about those tax codes, I assure you, I would have acquired a lot more real estate. To understand ultimate tax avoidance requires that you also to learn the power of real estate professional status.

To learn the origins of REPS, we must take you back to 1986.

In the realm of tax legislation, one of the most significant changes affecting real estate investors came with the Tax Reform Act of 1986. Signed into law by President Ronald Reagan, this landmark legislation introduced several reforms aimed at simplifying the tax code and closing loopholes. Among its many provisions, the act introduced stringent rules on passive activity losses, fundamentally changing how rental income and losses could be treated for tax purposes.

Before the Tax Reform Act of 1986, real estate investors enjoyed relatively lenient tax treatment. They could offset income from other sources, such as wages or business profits, with "losses" generated from real estate investments. For example, a real estate investor could have taxable income from a job and use $100,000 of depreciation to offset the income from his job. And voilà! This could result in NO TAXES!

This flexibility allowed high-income earners to significantly reduce their taxable income through strategic real estate investments, often leading to substantial tax shelters, and many were paying little or no taxes on their income.

However, by the mid-1980s, there was growing concern that these tax shelters were being abused, leading to substantial revenue losses for the government and creating an "unfair tax system" (lol, when has it ever been fair?).

The Tax Reform Act of 1986 aimed to address these issues by tightening the rules around passive activity losses, specifically around the losses from depreciation that could offset regular income.

KEY PROVISIONS OF THE TAX REFORM ACT OF 1986

The act introduced the concept of passive activity loss (PAL) rules. Passive activities were defined as business or trade activities in which the taxpayer does not materially participate. For most taxpayers, rental real estate activities were classified as passive activities.

The key provision was that losses from passive activities could only be used to offset income from other passive activities. This meant that passive losses could no longer be used to offset active income, such as wages or business income, or portfolio income, such as dividends and interest.

MATERIAL PARTICIPATION REQUIREMENT

The act defined "material participation" as regular, continuous, and substantial involvement in the operations of an activity. This requirement aimed to distinguish between active investors, who were genuinely involved in their business operations, and passive investors, who were not.

For example, an active investor that worked full-time in real estate was "materially participating" in the work and could therefore use the depreciation from real estate to offset all forms of income and effectively pay little-to-no taxes.

But a passive investor—like someone who worked for someone else as a full-time employee, perhaps (for example) working as a teacher—who owned a rental property was not "materially participating" in his real estate. He therefore could not offset the income from his job or the income from dividends.

But what if a teacher, or an attorney who didn't work in real estate, was married to someone who did qualify as a real estate professional? The result can only be described as tax alchemy, because it allows transforming taxable income into tax-free income.

So if someone is married to a real estate agent who qualifies for real estate professional status, they can benefit from additional tax benefits in several ways:

They then qualify for unlimited passive loss deductions: Normally, passive losses from rental properties are limited, but with REPS, these losses can offset other nonpassive income, potentially reducing taxable income from a job into 100% tax-free income.

They can also benefit from accelerated depreciation: The real estate professional can take full advantage of strategies like accelerated and bonus depreciation, which can further reduce taxable income by allowing larger deductions in the early years of property ownership, especially the additional depreciation in the first 5 to 15 years of owning a rental property.

Finally, expenses related to managing, maintaining, and improving rental properties can be fully deductible against other income, further lowering the overall tax bill.

Let's consider a simplified example to highlight the benefits and additional tax savings of being a real estate professional. Now, it is important to understand that you don't need to be a real estate agent to qualify for REPS; you just need to meet certain requirements defined by the IRS to qualify.

To qualify as a real estate professional, you must meet two key requirements:

- You must "materially participate" in the management of the property. This means you must spend more than 50% of your total working hours in real estate activities.
- You must spend at least 750 hours per year actively participating in real estate activities. These activities include managing properties, overseeing repairs, finding tenants, and doing other tasks directly related to the operation of real estate.

Remember, it is not necessary to get a real estate license to qualify for REP status; you qualify if you meet both requirements listed above.

Let's look at a scenario where a couple earns a W-2 income of $120,000.

They also receive dividend income of $10,000 and additional 1099 income of $20,000 from the commissions earned as a real estate agent (or they meet the two requirements).

Their rental losses due to depreciation, repairs, and other expenses are calculated at $25,000.

Without real estate professional status, the rental "losses" (aka depreciation) are considered passive and can only offset passive income, not active income (W-2s and 1099s) or investment income (interest and dividends). In this scenario, the

$25,000 rental loss cannot offset the $150,000 in W-2, dividend, and 1099 income.

The adjusted gross income is $120,000 (W-2) + $10,000 (dividends) + $20,000 (1099) = $150,000.

Assuming a 22% marginal tax rate, their tax liability would be about $16,500.

How about with real estate professional status?

The $25,000 rental loss can offset the $150,000 of combined W-2, dividend, and 1099 income.

Assuming everything else is the same, their income tax liability of $16,500 is reduced to $11,000 with REPS, saving about $5,500 in taxes!

The key to fully understanding the effectiveness of REPS is to also understand that W-2 income from a job is the highest form of all taxation, so you must find ways to convert your W-2 income into other forms of income that are taxed less than income from a job.

Let's delve deeper into a more detailed example of the tax savings with a couple earning $300,000 from a business they own.

> If they allocated $100,000 to wages and $200,000 to business income and received $38,000 in dividends, they would have a combined income of $338,000.
>
> They receive a rental income of $40,000 and can deduct expenses of $90,000 (the depreciation plus the repairs and miscellaneous expenses). This would result in a net rental loss of $50,000.
>
> What would it be without real estate professional status?

The combined income would be calculated as follows:

$100,000(W-2) + $38,000 (dividends) + $200,000 (K-1 Business) = $338,000.

The rental losses of $50,000 would not offset any of the current year income and would result in a higher taxable income.

Assuming a $30,000 standard deduction, the couple would be in the 24% marginal tax bracket with a tax liability of about $60,000.

How about with one spouse qualifying for REPS?

Now that one of the spouses qualifies for REP status, the rental losses of $50,000 can offset the taxable income, resulting in a reduced tax liability of $48,000.

The tax savings due to REPS is $60,000 – $48,000 = $12,000!

In this scenario, achieving real estate professional status results in a $12,000 reduction in tax liability, demonstrating significant tax savings and increased cash flow to reinvest in other assets.

Remember, achieving real estate professional status is like unlocking the ultimate tax cheat code for real estate investors. It can turn your rental income into tax-free gold, and it can also work magic on your dividends, W-2 income, and 1099 income. Imagine reinvesting those tax savings to buy even more properties—or stocks and ETFs—and then borrowing against them to fund your next big deal, all with money the IRS hasn't touched!

Unlock the ultimate tax cheat code: achieve real estate professional status to turn taxable income into tax-free wealth.

30

The Home Office Deduction

Your Tax-Saving Super Weapon

> **home of·fice**
> /hōm äfəs/
> *noun*
> a room or area in someone's home that they use to work
> at their job

Stella and I use every strategy we can find to reduce our tax bill—and so can you.

Here is our magic formula:

The Buy, Borrow, Die strategy +
business ownership + real estate investing

Anyone can do it, and this book is your guide. Soon you will be performing your own tax alchemy—transforming tax debts into tax refunds.

Here's how we've been working this magic:

- We bought our home using other people's money (OPM) with just 3% down. (And that translates to 97% tax-free!)
- We made sure to buy a home with a separate unit downstairs—"One to live in, one to rent out." Cha-ching!
- We furnished the downstairs unit so we could rent it out long term, mid term, or short term. We used 0% financing for five years to buy the furniture and appliances to increase our cash flow and decrease our taxes. Flexibility is key, right?
- We invest regularly using our iPhones, buying stocks and ETFs. And guess what? We're never going to sell those stocks and ETFs, which means we never pay taxes on the growth!
- We even use margin to borrow more for investing, creating tax-free money by simply pressing a button. Who knew that could be a thing?
- We're improving our property, and as inflation rises, so will the rents we are collecting. As the property rises in value (also tax-free), we will eventually take out a loan to build a guest house in the backyard. More tax-free rental income? Yes, please!
- When interest rates drop, we'll refinance it to a lower rate to boost our cash flow.
- Our next purchase? A lakeside property with the minimum down payment (more OPM = less taxes), fully furnished for short-term rental flexibility.

And this is just the tip of the iceberg. Doesn't this sound better than following the traditional advice: "Work hard, save money and pay your taxes?"

Now, let's talk about one of the biggest secrets to saving on your taxes: Section 280A of the IRS code. This section is your best friend if you use part of your home for business purposes or rent out a portion of it. Let me break it down.

THE HOME OFFICE DEDUCTION

Ever thought about deducting part of your home expenses because you work from home? You totally can! If you use a portion of your home exclusively and regularly for business, you can deduct a slice of your expenses. Think mortgage interest, property taxes, utilities, insurance, repairs—basically everything it costs to run your home.

The home office must be your principal place of business or where you regularly meet clients. Got it? Great!

RENTAL USE OF A DWELLING UNIT

Renting out a part of your home? You can deduct rental-related expenses too. (Special rules apply if the property is rented out for fewer than 15 days per year, allowing taxpayers to exclude rental income while still deducting related expenses. It's called the "Augusta Rule," and don't worry— it's covered later.) How's that for a sweet deal?

MIXED-USE PROPERTY

If your property is used both as a residence and for business or rental purposes, you'll need to prorate your expenses. So let's say 10% of your home is used as a home office; if that's the case, you can deduct 10% of your mortgage interest, property taxes, utilities, etc.

Let's make it real with an example:

Imagine your home is 2,000 square feet, and your home office takes up 200 square feet. That's 10% of your home. If your annual home expenses (including depreciation) add up to $23,640, you can deduct $2,360. Not bad, right?

And what about the rental property?

If you're renting out part of your home, like that downstairs unit we talked about, you can apply the same principles. If 40% of your home is rented out, that's a hefty deduction, especially if you're accelerating depreciation.

So whether you're a small business owner with a home office, a landlord renting out part of your home, or both, understanding and applying Section 280A can really cut down your tax bill. And who doesn't love keeping more of their hard-earned money?

Dreaming of buying a home with 100% OPM? Some credit unions make it possible with zero-down mortgages!

31

The Augusta Rule

Unlocking Tax-Free Income Through Short-Term Rentals

res·i·dence

/ˈrez(ə)d(ə)ns/

noun

a person's home; the place where someone lives

The Augusta Rule, also known as Section 280A(g) of the Internal Revenue Code is the same tax code that is used to reduce your tax bill using short-term rentals. This unique tax benefit **allows homeowners to earn rental income while paying no taxes on it.**

This provision can be particularly advantageous for business owners who can rent their home to their business for meetings or events, providing not only tax-free income, but also a business expense tax deduction for your business. That is worth repeating, "tax-free income for you AND a tax deduction for your business."

This chapter explains the Augusta Rule, how it works and how it can be leveraged for substantial tax savings, along with a simple example to illustrate its benefits.

UNDERSTANDING THE AUGUSTA RULE

Named after Augusta, Georgia—where homeowners famously rent out their homes during the Masters golf tournament—the Augusta Rule allows taxpayers to rent out their personal residence for up to 14 days per year **without having to report the rental income**.

The key points of the Augusta Rule are:

- **Residence.** You can rent out your home for up to 14 days per year and keep the income tax-free, as long as it's a house (or even an apartment, condo, motorhome, or houseboat, in certain circumstances) you've used within the calendar year as a residence, and you use the home for personal purposes for at least part of the year. (FYI, the days you can rent it out do NOT need to be consecutive, so you could rent out the house on the days that have the highest earning potential, for example, around holidays or special events.)
- **Tax-free income.** The rental income earned during this period is completely tax-free and does not need to be reported on the taxpayer's federal income tax return.
- **No deductible expenses.** While the income is tax-free, you cannot deduct any rental-related expenses, such as maintenance or depreciation.
- **Short-term rental.** The income is exempt from taxes ONLY if the total rental period for the residence is

less than 15 days within a calendar year. If you rent out the property for more than 14 days, then all the rental income (including the 14 days covered by the Augusta Code) from the property becomes taxable.

- **No self-rental.** The home can't be rented to or used by any of the residents of the property during the tax-exempt period, BUT it can be rented to an unrelated party or even to the taxpayer's own business (remember, businesses are a different entity from the people who own them) for events like meetings, conferences, or company retreats.
- **Documentation of the rental.** Proper documentation should be maintained, including rental agreements and proof of fair rental value (i.e., rate sheets for comparable properties and locations for the time[s] rented) to substantiate the rental arrangement.
- **Fair rental value.** The rate you charge for the rental must be a competitive rate based on the market for comparable properties (i.e., the same size and amenities) within the same market and for the same time period(s). Be sure to keep detailed records of rental rates near you for the days you rent the property, especially if you're charging high rates.

How can I also leverage the Augusta Rule as a business owner?

Once again, you can maximize your use of this tax code if you own real estate and you own a business.

The Augusta Rule can provide significant tax benefits by allowing you to rent your home to your business for short-term use. This rental income is tax-free, AND the business can deduct the rental expense as a legitimate business expense, no matter how much you rent your property for (as long as it's competitive and comparable to similar properties for the same dates).

If you have ever heard that "the tax codes are created by the rich for the rich," you are right. But you should also remember that the government has the power to change them—but it doesn't. The fact is that once the politicians learn about these tax codes, they will never close the loopholes, as they are using them themselves. Once again, if you can't beat 'em ... (Well, you know the rest.)

The good news is that you also know about Section 280A and the power of short-term rentals, which means you too can collect tax-free income! See? Anyone can become rich. Who knows, maybe one day we'll hang out at the Masters! (Figure 31-1 sums up the benefit nicely!)

FIGURE 31-1 Welcome to the Augusta Code, where your caddy carries your cash, not your clubs.

Let's consider a simple example to illustrate how the Augusta Rule can provide substantial tax-free income.

Let's use Sarah as our example, who is a current student of The Perfect Portfolio.

Sarah is not rich, but she does own a consulting business that she had been building for over 20 years. I would consider Sarah a HENRY—a High Earner, Not Rich Yet. She owns her primary residence in Indianapolis, Indiana, but I also learned that she also owns a vacation property she inherited when her father passed away.

Sarah's newly acquired house was not in Augusta, Georgia, but it was in Aiken, South Carolina, located just across the state line from Augusta. Her dad loved to ride horses and had purchased the home to be close to the equestrian center. She told me he never made much money and paid $90,000 for the home in 1992. She stays in the Aiken home a couple of months each year when she visits family, so it qualifies as a residence for her, even though she doesn't live there full-time.

We ran the numbers, and Sarah calculated that with the location and size of the house, the amenities (pool and spa, the equestrian center, and a short drive to Augusta), she could soon collect rent of approximately $5,500 a day if she rented the property during the Masters. Sarah was beyond excited!

I let her know that she could only do it for a maximum of 14 days and that she would have to coordinate with her CPA to fully document the rental. After estimating the average rents from March 31 to

April 13 , 2025, she placed listings for the property in a couple of vacation rental sites. Fortunately, we don't have to guess what the income would be, as it was booked immediately, and Sarah will receive about $77,000 of rent over the 14-day period. And the great news for Sarah is that she doesn't have to report any of the $77,000 on her taxes as income.

I love Sarah's next question: "Can I double dip?"

"What do you mean?" I asked.

Sarah clarified: "Can I collect the rent for the Aiken house for 14 days tax-free while I'm at my primary residence; then during the two weeks around the Indy 500, when rents are highest, can I rent my Indianapolis property for 14 days to my consulting business for an annual retreat and corporate get-together with my employees for both tax-free income and a business expense write-off?"

I smiled and said, "That's triple-dipping, Sarah."

Sarah laughed, responding, "I guess it is."

Sarah checked a few rental sites for comparable properties near her home and learned she could rent her Indianapolis house to her corporation for $2,550 per day, which placed her solidly within the range of choices for rentals during the Indy 500. That means she'll not only earn another $35,700 tax-free on top of the $77,000 tax-free she'll earn from the Aiken house, but she'll also get a $35,700 tax deduction for her business. That's a total of $112,700 TAX-FREE income AND $35,700 in business tax savings. Not too shabby, eh?

I then sent an email to my CPA, who sent Sarah the details. The email read:

Yes, a property owner can rent their property during the Masters Tournament (or another high-rent location) and receive income for up to 14 days without paying taxes on that income, according to IRS rules. This is often referred to as the "14-Day Rule" or "Augusta Rule." The rule allows homeowners to rent out their residence for up to 14 days per year without having to report the rental income on their tax return, meaning it is completely tax-free.

However, if the homeowner rents the property for more than 14 days in a year, the rental income from those additional days must be reported and all the days the property is rented become subject to taxation, including the first 14 days.

And so, Sarah set out to fully harness the power of the Augusta Rule—not just once, but twice—transforming her properties into income-generating machines while strategically sidestepping the taxman. With a tax-free windfall of $112,700 and an additional business tax deduction of $35,700, she's taking full advantage of a savvy financial loophole that's not just for the ultra-wealthy, but for anyone who owns real estate (a game-changer if you're also a business owner) and knows how to make the tax code work in their favor. The best part? She's enjoying the benefits of her properties while keeping more of her hard-earned money, right where it belongs—in her pocket.

It's stories like Sarah's that show how understanding the tax code can transform a financial plan. The beauty of the Augusta Rule is that it rewards those who think strategically, giving them the tools to double (or in Sarah's case, triple!) dip into tax-free income even without having millions of dollars or mega mansions.

Are you ready to see how much your properties can make you during high-demand events in your area? I know I'm already looking at the schedule of college football games near my house to see which ones create the highest demand for rentals (and the highest rental rates) near me.

"Triple-dipping" is possible, but always consult with a licensed tax professional.

32

The Short-Term Rentals Loophole

A Powerful Tool for Tax Savings

loop·hole

/ˈlo͞opˌ(h)ōl/

noun

an ambiguity or inadequacy in the law or a set of rules

Remember when I mentioned that Stella and I plan to save at least 1 million in taxes over the next 10 years? You might have had the thought, "That sounds impossible for me." But what if I told you, it's entirely within your reach? The first step is simple: DECIDE. Decide to create additional income streams, and then decide to learn how to legally avoid paying taxes on that income using the tax codes laid out here.

So have you made that decision? Remember, if you think you can, you're right. And if you think you can't . . . well, you're also right.

Let me take you back to a time when I was poor and decided I would do whatever it takes not to be poor anymore. There was no internet, no YouTube, and definitely no apps to help you buy and borrow and build wealth with the press of a button. Nobody in my neighborhood could explain how the rich pay no taxes, or explain how I could do it too.

Yet here I am today, with no college diploma, explaining advanced tax strategies to ordinary Americans—so you too can reduce your tax bill to ZERO.

WHAT'S THE SHORT-TERM RENTALS LOOPHOLE, AND WHY SHOULD YOU CARE?

One loophole every American should know about is the short-term rentals loophole, especially if you own "one to live in and one to rent." Short-term rentals have become a popular investment strategy, not just for the income they generate but also for the juicy tax benefits they offer.

Here's the best part: This loophole allows you to enjoy substantial tax savings without needing to qualify as a real estate professional (REP). Sound intriguing? Let's dive in and see how it works.

HOW DOES THE SHORT-TERM RENTALS LOOPHOLE WORK?

Usually, rental activities are considered passive, meaning losses from these activities can only offset other passive income. But what if I told you there's a way to turn your short-term rental into a nonpassive activity? By doing so, you can use any losses to offset your active income—like your wages or business income—and keep more of your hard-earned cash.

Want to know how? Let's explore the criteria.

WHAT MAKES A RENTAL ACTIVITY NONPASSIVE?

To classify your short-term rental as nonpassive, you need to meet two key conditions:

- **Average rental period.** The average period of customer use for the property must be 7 days or less. Alternatively, it can be 30 days or less if you provide significant personal services. Do you think you could manage that?
- **Material participation.** You need to be actively involved in managing the property. The IRS gives you several ways to prove this, like spending more than 100 hours on the activity, with no one else spending more time than you. Does that sound doable?

By meeting these criteria, you can classify your short-term rental as nonpassive. This means you can offset rental losses against your active income—leading to more tax-free income in your pocket. How good does that sound?

REPS VS THE SHORT-TERM RENTAL LOOPHOLE: WHAT'S THE DIFFERENCE?

Now, you might be wondering how this compares with real estate professional status. Let's recap:

Real estate professional status:

- Requires you to spend more than 50% of your total working hours and at least 750 hours per year in real estate activities. Do you have that kind of time?
- Allows rental losses to offset active income if you materially participate in your rental activities.

Short-term rentals loophole:

- Requires shorter average rental periods (7 days or less, or 30 days or less with significant services) and material participation.
- Does not need to meet the 50% and 750-hour thresholds.
- Allows rental losses to offset active income without needing to qualify as a real estate professional.

A SIMPLE EXAMPLE TO BRING IT HOME

Let's say you have a W-2 income of $150,000 and you've purchased a property for $500,000 to use as a short-term rental, generating $50,000 in rental income. After accounting for expenses—including a $100,000 depreciation deduction (using cost segregation and bonus depreciation), mortgage interest, maintenance, and other costs—you end up with $150,000 in total expenses, resulting in a net short-term rental loss of $100,000.

Without the Short-Term Rentals Loophole

- The $100,000 loss cannot offset your $150,000 of W-2 income because it's considered passive.
- Taxable income: $150,000 (W-2 income) − $14,600 (standard deduction) = $135,400.
- Tax on $135,400 for a single person is $25,538.

With the Short-Term Rentals Loophole

- The $100,000 short-term rental loss offsets your W-2 income.
- Taxable income: $150,000 (W-2 income) − $100,000 (rental loss) − $14,600 (standard deduction) = $35,400.
- Tax on $35,400 for a single person is $4,016.

How much do you save? $25,538 − $4,016 = **$21,522 in tax savings!**

WHY YOU SHOULD CONSIDER THE SHORT-TERM RENTALS LOOPHOLE

The short-term rentals loophole is a powerful tax-saving strategy for real estate investors. By meeting the criteria for nonpassive short-term rentals, you can significantly reduce your taxable income, leading to substantial tax savings and more tax-free cash for investing.

So let me ask you: Are you ready to take advantage of this loophole and start shrinking your tax bill? It's all about making S.M.A.R.T. decisions and using the tools available to you.

Are you in?

Use the REPStracker app to track your short-term rental and long-term rental hours.

33

House Hacking

Transforming Your Home from
Liability to Tax-Free Asset

as·set

/ˈaˌset/

noun

any useful thing, or something that holds value

If you've spent any time on YouTube, you've probably heard advice such as, "You should buy assets, not liabilities, and a home is not an asset."

While statements like this might make you think twice about buying a house, I'm here to tell you that this advice can be misleading—especially if you're currently renting when you could be buying.

Let's break it down. Imagine you could have bought a home five years ago for around $320,000. Fast-forward to today, and that same home might be worth about $495,000! With just a 3% down payment—around $10,000—you could have locked in a mortgage payment of about $1,700 a month. And here's a bonus: Once you factor in tax savings from mortgage interest, you'd get about $3,000 a year back, bringing that monthly payment down to $1,450. Now, what if I told you there was a way to make that payment even lower? Or better yet—what if your home could pay YOU?

This is where house hacking comes in. But before we dive in, let me ask you: Wouldn't it be nice if your house could help cover your bills? What if you could live in a home that others help you pay for? Let's explore this strategy that can springboard you toward tax savings while building your wealth.

THE COST OF WAITING

The worst advice I've heard about real estate is "Rent, don't buy." And as we noted before, "Wait until you have 20% down" is equally bad advice. But if you're renting now, you might find yourself in a tough spot. Average rents have shot up from about $1,450 to around $2,000 a month. And here's the kicker: If you live in a high-tax state, you're paying rent with money that's already been taxed—meaning that $2,000 rent might really be costing you $2,600!

So here's a question for you: Is waiting worth it? What if home prices keep rising? As I mentioned previously, I predict that in the next ten years, homes in desirable areas might double in value again. But don't just take my word for it—let's consider a few key factors.

WHY PRICES KEEP GOING UP

First, interest rates. As I'm writing this book, the Federal Reserve is lowering rates. What happens then? Loans get cheaper, more people can afford to buy, and prices go up. More buyers = more competition = higher home prices.

Second, corporate landlords. Did you know that corporations, institutional investors, and LLCs own about 575,000 single-family homes? Imagine trying to buy in a neighborhood where these big players are also shopping. Think you can outbid them?

Third, migration. People are flocking to states with low taxes, low crime, and good job opportunities. What happens when everyone wants to live in the same few places? You guessed it—prices soar even more.

HOUSE HACKING 101

Now, let's talk about house hacking—my favorite way to turn a home from a liability into an asset. Stella and I used this in Tennessee. We didn't just buy any house. We searched for one with at least five bedrooms and three bathrooms. Why? Because we wanted to rent out part of it.

Oh, and if you're reading this from Tennessee, don't worry—we were warned not to "California your Tennessee," and we promise, we won't!

Think about this: Would you buy a home if you knew someone else would cover most of your mortgage? We did, and it worked! We rented out part of our home to a traveling nurse, and that rent covers most of our mortgage. Plus we get tax benefits like depreciation and running a business from home.

So do you want to pay less in taxes? Maybe even zero? House hacking is your new best friend. (See Figure 33-1 for what it is not!)

FIGURE 33-1   This is definitely *not* what we meant by "house hacking."

THE FUTURE OF HOUSE HACKING

We're always looking for ways to increase income and reduce taxes. Right now, I'm researching "Boxabl"—a company that makes tiny homes. We're on the waitlist, and we're also comparing tiny homes from Home Depot. Our plan? Add a guest house to our property and rent it out for even more tax-free income!

And here's a question to ponder: If you could turn your home into a moneymaking machine, wouldn't you want to do it over and over again? That's our plan—buy another property, hack it, and let the income flow in while we pay very little in taxes.

Yes, a home can be a liability if it just takes money out of your pocket. But what if you could flip the script? What if, instead of following the old advice to "only buy a home with

20% down," you bought a home as soon as you could and used house hacking to turn it into an asset?

So here's my challenge to you: Buy a home, but don't just buy any home. Find one that you can hack. Use the strategies in this book to slash your tax bill—maybe even down to zero!

Are you ready to transform your home from a liability into a tax-free asset?

Let's get hacking!

Combine house hacking with the short-term rentals loophole! Cha-ching!

PART THREE

Income and Asset Protection

The Third Pillar of a
Buy, Borrow, Die Strategy

The Five Pillars

34

Maximizing the Benefits of Term Life Insurance

Protecting Wealth with Smart Riders

> **rid·er**
>
> /ˈrīdər/
>
> *noun*
>
> an adjustment or an add-on to a basic insurance policy.
> Riders are designed to provide additional benefit over
> the stated coverage in the basic policy

I get it—life insurance isn't exactly exciting. But trust me, understanding it is crucial to your overall wealth-building and protection strategy.

If you need a deep dive into life insurance, check out *Top 25 Ways an IUL Can Secure Your Financial Future: And Build a Tax-Free Family Bank*. It covers all types of insurance and breaks down the pros and cons of term vs permanent insurance.

Now, here's a quick recap of life insurance basics:

There are two main types: "term" and "perm."

Term insurance is temporary and the cheapest way to get the most coverage for the least amount of money, usually for 10–30 years. It's typically used to replace income if something happens to a breadwinner.

Term is a great value, but keep in mind—it's only "cheap" because it expires. When it does, so do your premiums.

I recommend that most Americans buy term insurance for affordable coverage over 20–30 years. But it's also smart to consider adding some permanent insurance for when the term runs out.

Remember, you can only buy life insurance while you're healthy, and it gets more expensive as you age. So lock in both term and perm insurance while you're young and in good health.

Now, term insurance used to be pretty straightforward, but things have changed. The good news is that the tax advantages are the same: When you die, your family gets the death benefit 100% tax-free. But what happens if you don't die and instead get seriously ill?

That's where life insurance "riders" come in (see Figure 34-1). Riders are optional add-ons to customize your policy to fit your needs.

Let's talk about three important "accelerated death benefit riders." These allow access to cash if you're diagnosed with a terminal, chronic, or critical illness, letting you use the money for medical expenses or other needs.

When reviewing your term policy, make sure it includes these four essential riders, which I'll help you remember with the acronym "TCCC."

FIGURE 34-1   Insurance riders don't need to be confusing (or confused, like these guys).

- Terminal illness rider
- Chronic illness rider
- Critical illness rider
- Convertibility rider (so you can switch to permanent insurance later)

These riders come at no extra cost unless you use them, so it's worth checking your policy for them.

These TCCC riders can allow you to advance the death benefit to help pay for your care and/or replace income if you experience a terminal illness or a chronic illness or become critically ill. The money can be used to cover medical expenses, pay off debts, or handle other financial needs during the policyholder's remaining life. The amount that is advanced is typically deducted from the total death benefit, with the remaining amount passed to your heirs. The advance of the death benefit is tax-free, and so is the remaining death benefit.

A terminal illness rider on a term life insurance policy allows the policyholder to access a portion of the death benefit early if the holder is diagnosed with a terminal illness and given a limited time to live, usually 6 to 12 months.

A chronic illness rider can pay income to your family if you need help in your home with your activities of daily living (ADLs). This is like purchasing long-term care (LTC) insurance, but for a fraction of the price. Most people think that long-term care is only for old people, but I've had clients that have used these riders in their 40s and 50s, after they have a stroke or when they get terminally ill with cancer. These riders can help provide an improved quality of life—while lessening the burden on family and/or friends to take care of them.

A critical illness rider can advance the death benefit if you're diagnosed with a covered critical illness, such as cancer, heart attack, or stroke. The rider can pay out a lump sum or regular payments depending on the company offering the rider.

A convertibility rider means you should have the option of converting your term to a permanent life insurance policy, if needed, without having a medical exam. This may be important if you get sick later in life and learn your term insurance is at risk of lapsing. You would be able to convert your term policy to a permanent life insurance policy even if you are not insurable. It typically can be converted up until age 65.

One thing to keep an eye on: There are a lot of ways to "lose money" with life insurance.

You can lose all your past premiums if/when your term insurance expires worthless. But you can also "lose" money by paying for more expensive permanent insurance over 10–30 years when you could have been paying for less expensive term insurance, so you must decide how much should be "term" and how much should be "perm."

And don't forget: Be sure your term insurance includes all the benefits of TCCC.

In the chapters ahead, we're going to explore the wave of tax increases rolling out across the country—especially for those without long-term care insurance. Here's something most people don't realize: Long-term care insurance isn't just about protecting your assets; it's also a smart strategy for reducing taxes.

Don't worry, we'll break it all down for you in the upcoming chapters!

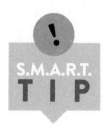

Text "OPM" to (833) 455-4540 for free chapters from my best-selling book about using life insurance for growing, protecting, and maximizing assets.

35

Indexed Universal Life Insurance

The Swiss Army Knife of Investing and Tax Avoidance

> **Swiss ar·my knife**
>
> /swis ˈärmē nīf/
>
> *noun*
>
> multifunction pocketknife or multitool, having a blade and various tools, such as screwdrivers and can openers

When I met with Jane a second time, she immediately thanked me once again, saying "Mark, I can't tell you how incredible it feels to not have any credit card debt. And rather than invest $900 a month, I've started investing the $225 weekly into my M1 account as you suggested. It is fun to watch it grow week to week, knowing that the growth is tax-free, and I never plan to sell it. You have really changed my life already."

"This is what I do for fun," I responded with a smile.

"So, Mark, what's next?" Jane asked.

"Well, it depends," I said. What's your next goal, now that you are free of the credit card debt?"

Jane replied: "I'd like to review how I'm going to retire, and I'm also concerned about the need for long-term care. I'd like to get my mother long-term care, but I don't think she will qualify with her health issues. Knowing what she's been dealing with, and how expensive it's been, I've been thinking that I should purchase LTC while I'm still in good health. I've also seen some friends be forced to liquidate their assets to pay for their parents' care."

"I know your concerns very well," I sympathized. "When both my parents got sick, my mother was there to take care of my dad, but when my dad passed away, my mom had to rely on her kids for almost everything, to buy groceries, take her to doctor appointments, and provide financial and emotional support. Her care was expensive for the time she had to spend in a care facility. Fortunately, today the cost of long-term care has become more affordable with some innovation in the insurance industry."

I gave Jane a copy of my book about indexed universal life insurance (IUL), *Top 25 Ways an IUL Can Secure Your Financial Future,* and asked her to read it.

"Let's cover the basics," I said. "Sound good?"

"Sounds great," Jane answered.

"There is term insurance," I told her, "which I may recommend if you need more insurance, but term doesn't have a real long-term care rider; and as you know, it will eventually lapse. The least expensive option I've found for buying LTC is when buying an IUL policy and adding an LTC rider. But only a handful of IUL policies in the market have real LTC, so it is important to know the difference between the policy types and which riders they have."

I continued, "All permanent insurance has a cash value or savings component, and the policy's cash value grows without taxes, and you can access that cash value via loans or withdrawals tax-free, at any age. When you die, the death benefit is passed to your heirs tax-free."

I then explained that I wouldn't suggest universal life (UL) or whole life (WL) insurance, because though they typically earn a rate of return that is tax-free, that return barely keeps ahead of inflation. Earning 5% return minus 4% for inflation leaves you with a net return of 1% per year. I understand that may be better than your taxable savings account, but it is still impossible to get ahead after adjusting for inflation.

I also explained that there are Variable Universal Life (VUL) insurance policies, which are essentially like investing in a mutual fund wrapped inside a life insurance policy—offering the potential for tax-free gains.

"A VUL can be a good tool for tax avoidance," I said, "but just like a mutual fund, it is like riding a roller coaster—the ups can be both exciting and exhilarating, and the downs can cause fear and anxiety, especially when the talking heads are discussing the coming of the next financial Armageddon.

"Personally, I own a VUL that I purchased in 2005, but I only continue funding it for the permanent life insurance. I want assets that won't crash, so I can borrow from them when I see an opportunity, and the great thing about an IUL is that it grows when the market rises but can't crash when the market does."

Jane looked confused. "How does an IUL go up with the market but can't crash when the market does?" she asked.

I filled Jane in on the following: As I mention in the book, IUL was created in 1997 when some genius put a risk-free investment, called a "market-linked CD," inside a life insurance policy. Once sheltered inside a life insurance policy, risk-free and tax-free investing was born. I look at IUL as the Swiss army knife of investing, since it has many more features than any other type of life insurance policy (see Figure 35-1).

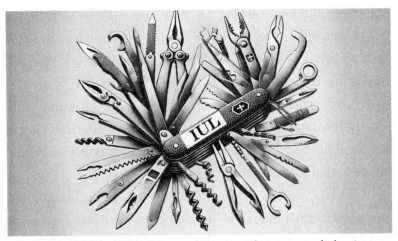

FIGURE 35-1   The IUL might not have quite this many tools, but it sure feels like it.

There are a lot of critics who scream about the "fees" of permanent life insurance and always push the "Buy Term and Invest the Difference" strategy. These same folks are often the ones who recommend investing in 401(k)s and paying off all debt. Sure, that can work for some, but it's a tougher road to building wealth, especially when battling inflation and taxes.

Now, where do the critics and I agree? We agree on this:

"Life insurance is not an investment!"

Yep, that's true. Legally, it's not. But here's the twist—you can shelter your money inside a life insurance policy, grow it 100% tax-free, and pass it on tax-free too.

You'll also hear, "You only get the death benefit and lose the cash value when you die." That's true with whole life, but not with IUL. With IUL, your cash value adds to your death benefit. So your heirs get both—100% tax-free.

Critics would probably disagree with me here, but I think most people following the Buy Term and Invest the Difference strategy will likely work until they die or run out of money in retirement. Why? Because that strategy only focuses on investing and ignores the power of using other people's money (OPM).

The strategy is clear: You buy your investments with your money and invest for the long haul in mutual funds and retirement accounts. And perhaps one day you can retire when you are 65 or 70, and *hopefully* you won't run out of money during your retirement years. Hopefully? Really?

Personally, I think of owning an IUL like having a tax-free family bank—for buying and borrowing, aka Buy, Borrow, Die, and using the loans for investing in other assets.

For example, you can buy and borrow many times.

You can fund a brokerage account and purchase stocks and ETFs with the plan of never selling them to avoid the capital gains taxes.

Rather than sell them, you can take a margin loan from the brokerage account to fund your monthly/annual life insurance premiums, which is funding your tax-advantaged life insurance policy with money that has never been taxed.

You may have a long-term plan to borrow from your life insurance policy to purchase real estate or borrow to buy more stocks/ETFs after a market crash, aka "buy low, never sell." And when the stocks/ETFs recover after the crash, you could borrow again using a margin loan to buy other assets or fund your IUL.

In the meantime, a properly structured Indexed Universal Life (IUL) policy can provide you with permanent life insurance and the additional benefits of TCC riders—Terminal Illness, Chronic Illness, and Critical Illness. Since it's a permanent policy, it doesn't need a convertibility rider (the "C" in TCCC). Make sure to do your research, though, because not all riders are available in all states.

After I did a quick review of Jane's assets and liabilities and answered some more questions about riders, Jane decided to apply for an inexpensive 20-year term insurance policy with the TCCC riders—Terminal Illness, Chronic Illness, Critical Illness, and Convertibility. Additionally, she chose to apply for a $250,000 IUL to provide some permanent coverage, to which she added the LTC (Long-Term Care) rider. I explained to her that adding the LTC rider could provide her with up to $5,000 a month to pay for LTC expenses if she ever needed it. If she didn't use it, the unused portion would be passed to her heirs as part of the death benefit.

"What about retirement?" Jane asked.

"Well, Jane," I said, "you are already building your retirement when you are funding your brokerage account. Just because it is not called a 'retirement account' doesn't mean you can't retire with it.

"Keep investing the $225 per week into your brokerage account, and let's create a plan so you own at least two pieces of real estate.

"We can also have you start investing in a portfolio focused on high dividends, which builds income that can be collected at any age, if needed.

I have multiple portfolios, but my current dividend-focused portfolio on M1 Finance is worth about $163,000 as of today, and it generates monthly dividend income. The portfolio produces around $3,500 per month, and because I'm also buying more shares each week, the income will continue to grow. I am also using margin to buy additional shares since the dividends are around 26%, and I'm borrowing at less than 6%. The growth of my account is accelerating because I'll never sell, and I'm currently reinvesting all the dividends to buy more shares. I'll borrow from the portfolio, but only to create more income streams and/ or create tax deductions. Doesn't that sound better than a traditional retirement account?"

Jane agreed, "Yes, it does."

"Great," I said. "I'll send you an email with the recording of our latest classes, where I go over the positions I hold in my brokerage account, including why I also invest in Bitcoin and precious metals. The classes explain how these assets can help fight inflation—especially when using them for buying and borrowing. From there, you can decide if diversifying with the same strategies while building your dividend income makes sense for you."

It's funny—if you tell someone that you get $3,500 a month in dividend income from $163,000, they will tell you that is impossible!

Does everything I do sound impossible? Maybe—but only if you haven't read this book. For those who have, it's just common sense.

INDEXED UNIVERSAL LIFE INSURANCE: THE SWISS ARMY KNIFE OF TAX AVOIDANCE

Now that we have covered how even a "cheap" term insurance policy can help you with asset protection when adding the TCCC riders to your policy, and how an IUL can get you inexpensive LTC coverage and let you invest without the risk of loss, let's cover how an IUL can also help you to avoid future tax increases.

Depending on your age, you may recall when the government started mandating that all Americans must buy auto insurance in the 1970s or pay a tax/penalty if you didn't. This expanded across the country and was before my time, but I do remember when the government mandated that all Americans must purchase health insurance, and if they didn't, they would also face a tax/penalty. It was in 2010 when we learned about the Affordable Care Act, which went into effect in 2014.

This mandate also made it illegal for an insurance company to deny someone coverage if they had a preexisting condition. I had mixed feelings about paying another tax penalty, but my parents had preexisting health conditions, and when I became uninsurable myself, at age 40, I was grateful I was able to still purchase health insurance. So are the 20+ million Americans that also have a preexisting condition and would likely be pushed into bankruptcy without health insurance.

The thing to remember is that the government typically provides tax deductions to incentivize the activities that it wants to encourage, like donating to a church or charity, which provide a benefit to us all and to the community.

The government also penalizes the activities that may put a financial burden on the rest of us, such as smoking and drinking, which can cause the rest of us to pay higher health insurance premiums.

The Affordable Care Act was a double-edged sword: It prevented many from falling into poverty after a medical emergency from a preexisting condition. But it also increased the cost of health insurance (after all, the quickest way to increase the cost of anything is to get the government involved) by removing the incentive to stop smoking or drinking (heavily), and in some ways rewarded smokers by giving them the same rates as nonsmokers.

Fortunately, life insurance is an even playing field. It rewards those of us with "healthy habits" with lower premiums, and penalizes those that use tobacco or drink too much with higher premiums.

So this begs the question, why does the government apply the largest "penalty" when working? Does the government not want us to work?

Well, yes, sort of. The government only penalizes those that only know how to make money from working at a regular job. They can't tax the rich, as they have access to the best lawyers, best accountants, and best tax advice. The good news is that many are using Buy, Borrow Die to pay no taxes, and now you can easily do that too. You can also learn all the tax codes used by the rich to legally cut down your tax bill to ZERO.

New tax penalties are being introduced for individuals who don't secure legitimate long-term care (LTC) coverage. These penalties could also apply to those with IUL policies that include TCC riders, as they do not qualify as true LTC coverage. To avoid these penalties and ensure you're fully protected, it's critical to choose a policy that includes a legal and qualified LTC rider. These LTC mandates are already being rolled out in many states, and future taxes may target anyone with a whole life or IUL policy that lacks a proper LTC rider. Protect yourself now by ensuring your policy meets the legal requirements for LTC coverage.

Since it's only the state of Washington that currently applies this mandate/penalty, and we don't know which states will be next to add the mandate, you will have to see if the state you live in is next on the list. But I'm sure it won't surprise you that the states with the highest taxes already are leading the way, with California, Hawaii, and New York getting ready to join Washington in rolling out the mandate and/or penalty.

COST VS VALUE

"So, Mark, what is the cost of the LTC rider vs the state-mandated LTC?"

Good question! As I mentioned, it's only Washington State that started this tax in 2023, with the "WA Cares Fund," which requires employees to contribute 0.58% of their wages, with no cap on the taxable income.

The program provides up to $36,500 in lifetime benefits for long-term care needs such as in-home care and nursing home care.

Trust me, this is a huge tax, with virtually no benefit to the residents of Washington State. Assuming a $100,000 taxable income, the WA Cares Fund tax would be about $580 a year, for a maximum lifetime benefit of $36,500. In my opinion, this is robbery!

In comparison, a long-term care rider added to an IUL can cost 10 or 20 bucks a month and can provide a $250,000 or even a $500,000 lifetime benefit. This, of course, would vary depending on your age and health, but charging 200–400% for 1/10th of the benefit demonstrates the government's consistent track record for "efficiency."

Remember, the poor don't pay any taxes, and neither do the rich. It is only the average Americans that follow the average advice that pay their unfair share.

TERM OR PERM?

I'm not here to tell you what to do with your money.

If after reading this, you only want to "Buy Term and Invest the Difference," that is your choice. This is a free country (for now).

But I also believe that implementing a Buy, Borrow, Die strategy will be far more effective—especially when buying life insurance, then borrowing to purchase stocks and ETFs after a crash, or borrowing to buy real estate, or even borrowing to start a business.

QUADRUPLE TAX-FREE?

It is important to remember that life insurance is typically funded with after-tax dollars.

This means that most Americans will go to work, fight inflation and taxes, and then fund their life insurance from what is left *after* Uncle Sam takes a bite.

What if after reading this book, you began funding a brokerage account with stocks and ETFs, and you decide to take a
margin loan (which can be used for any purpose) but you chose
to pay your life insurance premiums with it? Since life insurance is triple-tax protected, you are funding a tax-free asset with
money that has never been taxed!

It is like having your cake and eating it too, but this time the
government didn't eat 30–50% of your cake first.

Don't let the government eat your cake.

PART FOUR

Cryptocurrency

*The Fourth Pillar of a
Buy, Borrow, Die Strategy*

The Five Pillars

36

Bitcoin vs Bucks

*Why Digital Coins Beat the
Unlimited Dollar Machine*

> **cryp·to·cur·ren·cy**
>
> /ˈkrɪpˌtōˌkərənsē/
>
> *noun*
>
> a digital currency in which transactions are verified and
> records maintained by a decentralized system using
> cryptography, rather than by a centralized authority

CRYPTOCURRENCY

As of November 2023, interest in Bitcoin and Bitcoin ETFs (discussed in the next chapter) has skyrocketed. Americans have invested over $100 billion into ETFs that hold Bitcoin, and this figure doesn't include the surge in direct purchases of Bitcoin (BTC) itself. If you've never thought of owning Bitcoin, I fully understand why you might not want to own it. After all, the pundits are loud and opinionated (as they usually are):

"Bitcoin is purely digital and is backed by nothing. It's a Ponzi scheme."

Which may leave you wondering, "So who owns Bitcoin, and why would they invest in a "Ponzi scheme"?

According to the National Institute of Retirement Security, about 72% of Millennials (ages 26–41) are concerned they won't be able to live comfortably and achieve a financially secure retirement. It is also interesting to learn that this same group also owns around 26% of the Bitcoin that exists today (worth about $322 billion at today's prices), making them the most active generation to adopt cryptocurrency in their investment strategy. This group also tends to be more tech-savvy and more open to new financial technologies, driving the highest adoption rate.

Bitcoin ownership among Gen X (ages 42–57) is lower compared with Millennials, with about 14% of this generation holding Bitcoin. This group is generally more conservative in their investment strategies, but still shows a growing interest in cryptocurrencies.

What is also very interesting is that Millennials and Generation Z are also the generations that tend to trust Wall Street and banks the least. Several surveys and studies have shown that these younger generations have significant skepticism toward traditional financial institutions. Yes, I'm obviously one of them, having authored *Rich Man, Poor Bank: What the banks don't want you to know about money*. Yes, today I still advocate for using credit unions over megabanks, because credit unions are not-for-profit financial co-ops, which keep the money within your community rather than funneling it back to Wall Street.

Then there are the Baby Boomers (ages 58–76): Bitcoin ownership is even lower among Baby Boomers, with a smaller percentage involved in cryptocurrency investments. This generation tends to favor more traditional investment vehicles like stocks and bonds. This generation is fully invested in a strategy known as "Buy a diversified portfolio of mutual funds in your 401(k)." (Yup. There is that gag reflex, again!)

My wish and my hope is that the folks who are invested in that strategy read this book to evaluate the effectiveness and tax efficiency of their strategy.

I find it very interesting that when Bitcoin was born, we were also in the Great Recession, which was the cause of the greatest housing collapse and largest stock market crash since the Great Depression. I also find it massively suspicious that those who were responsible for the causes of those financial meltdowns are some of the same people that also call Bitcoin a "Ponzi scheme."

Let's take a deep dive to educate you with more facts about Bitcoin and see if the pundits and talking heads on the (fake) news are right.

Bitcoin was conceptualized in 2008 by an unknown individual (or group of individuals) using the pseudonym **Satoshi Nakamoto**. The white paper (a detailed report), titled "Bitcoin: A Peer-to-Peer Electronic Cash System," outlined a decentralized digital currency that would operate without a central authority, leveraging blockchain (a decentralized, digital ledger that records transactions across a network of computers, ensuring transparency and security without the need for a central authority) technology to enable secure, transparent, and immutable transactions.

On January 3, 2009, Nakamoto (identity still unknown today) mined the first block of the Bitcoin blockchain, known as the "Genesis Block" or "Block 0," embedded with the message: **"The Times 03/Jan/2009 Chancellor on brink of second bailout for banks."** This message underscored the motivation behind Bitcoin's creation: to offer an alternative to centralized financial systems, which are prone to crisis and corruption.

In the early days, Bitcoin was a niche fascination among cryptography enthusiasts—a bit like a secret club for people who really loved solving puzzles. Cryptography, the science behind Bitcoin, isn't just about secret codes. It's the method we use to secure communication and data, keeping it safe from prying eyes. Imagine it like turning your plain message into a scrambled code (ciphertext), so only someone with the right key can unscramble it.

This is what protects sensitive information in everything from online banking to cryptocurrency. It ensures that there is privacy, data integrity, and only the right people get access to what matters. So next time you're making a financial transaction or sending a message, cryptography is quietly working behind the scenes, making sure no one else can sneak a peek at your information.

The earliest adopters of Bitcoin—like Hal Finney, who received the first Bitcoin transaction from Nakamoto, and others in the "Cypherpunk" community—played crucial roles in developing and promoting the technology. The first real-world Bitcoin transaction occurred on May 22, 2010, when Laszlo Hanyecz paid 10,000 Bitcoin for two pizzas, marking the currency's first entry into the broader economy as "money." (As a painful side note, 10,000 Bitcoin at today's price is $636,113,721.89! Talk about some expensive pizzas!)

In 2013, a new company that offered digital currency investments to institutional and accredited investors (a fancy way of saying it was only offered to the rich) formed the Grayscale Bitcoin Trust (symbol GBTC), a forward-thinking investment vehicle that would provide investors with exposure to Bitcoin without the need to directly purchase or store the cryptocurrency. These early investors were fortunate indeed, as Bitcoin was about $125 at the time and soon skyrocketed to around $750 at the peak at the end of 2014. It then saw a rapid decline, and by the end of 2014, it was around $300.

It was May of 2015 before the average American could easily purchase Bitcoin, when the Grayscale Bitcoin Trust was publicly traded and investors could buy GBTC in a regular brokerage account. Finally, even ordinary Americans could have exposure to Bitcoin, without the complexities of buying and storing Bitcoin. These early adopters in the so-called Ponzi scheme saw the price of Bitcoin go from $300 in a coin to as high as $20,000 by the end of 2017.

I think it's also very important to underscore that there have been crashes after these massive spikes in the price, when many new investors were buying Bitcoin at any price. This caused many investors to "buy very high and sell very low." (I highly recommend you don't use this strategy. lol)

I made my first purchase of Bitcoin on August 10th of 2017 when the price was $3,446.74. (Can you imagine buying Bitcoin that cheap today?) I honestly don't remember who told me about it, but when I heard about a decentralized financial system (not controlled by Wall Street), it was all I needed to hear. I was 100% all in!

I began researching and buying Bitcoin, but also buying dozens of other cryptocurrencies on multiple exchanges. Around that same time, driven by fear of missing out (FOMO), Bitcoin hit an all-time high (ATH) of around $19,500 by December 17th. Many of these unlucky investors who bought at that high then watched as their BTC crashed to a low of $3,200 by December of 2018. For investors that bought at the top and sold at the bottom, they experienced an **84% loss**—brutal!

Bitcoin then began another bull run, reaching an ATH of around $20,000 by December of 2019. Just as these BTC investors began singing, "I'M GONNA BE RICH . . . ," BTC began another steep decline down to $3,300 in February of 2019.

Bitcoin then went into a bull run, hitting a new ATH of $64,895 by April of 2021. And again . . . "I'M GONNA BE RICH . . ." before the next decline back down to around $17,000 by December of 2022.

This seems like a good time to mention a term use by Bitcoin investors: "HODL." HODL originally came from a typo in an internet post back in 2013 when someone was typing too fast when they were trying to type "hold" as they mentioned how they were going to hold their Bitcoin for the long term. Since then, the cryptocurrency world has embraced it, and HODL now stands for "hold on for dear life!"—implying not selling even when markets go down or become volatile.

As of March of 2024, Bitcoin hit a new ATH of around $73,000. It has been quite the ride, but I have a simple plan, very similar to my plan of when I buy stock, ETFs, and real estate. I'm going to "HODL" and always buy more. I plan to buy BTC the rest of my life. If the prices drop, I'll buy even more, and I plan to never sell it.

Yes, you can also buy, and then borrow (tax-free) secured by your BTC using a company called "SALT Lending," which allows users to leverage their cryptocurrency holdings as collateral for loans. SALT is an acronym for "Secured Automated Lending Technology."

"But wait, Mark, what if Bitcoin is a Ponzi scheme? After all, it's virtual and not backed by anything."

Let's reflect all the way back to Chapter 3, when we asked, "What is money?" and compared it with the paper in your wallet. Does printing a piece of paper and adding the words "FEDERAL RESERVE NOTE" on it make it money? Especially when most of the "money" is made virtually (by pressing buttons) in a computer?

Remember, to identify money, you must identify the three characteristics of money.

1.   Enough people agree it has value.
2.   It must be easily transferable.
3.   And it must be in **limited supply**.

So let's compare Federal Reserve notes (aka the US dollars in your wallet that have numbers printed on them) with Bitcoin and see which has the characteristics of money.

Can enough people identify the US dollar as money?
Yes, they can. We can check that box.

Is the US dollar easily transferable?
Well not the paper, but remember, most of the money is created as simple bank entries, anyway. It is almost totally virtual. (There are currently about 2.3 TRILLION U.S. dollars in the form of physical cash—either printed as paper money or minted

as coins—but approximately 21 TRILLION U.S. dollars exist in total, most of which are digital entries on computers.) Since they are created in a computer, they can be transferred easily by a computer. So we can also check that box.

Is the US dollar in limited supply?

No, it isn't. The government prints it like it's toilet paper. (Actually, I was talking with a friend of mine recently, and we calculated that toilet paper has held its value over the last 20 years better than the US dollar has, so maybe we should say they "print it like dollars"?)

How about Bitcoin? Does it pass these tests?

Do enough people agree that Bitcoin has value?

Yes, they do, and because they agree it has value, it is worth around $95,000 today. Over 180 million people around the world agree on that.

In fact, Venezuela (after it devalued its worthless paper currency, the bolivar, so fast that it couldn't even afford to buy toilet paper with it) so strongly agrees that Bitcoin is money that it now uses Bitcoin as its primary currency. The Central African Republic also uses Bitcoin as its primary currency, as it also could no longer afford toilet paper with its Central African francs.

Is Bitcoin in limited supply?

Yes, it is. So we can check that box too.

How limited is the supply of Bitcoin? Well, there will only be 21 million ever in existence, and only 450 new BTC can be created by mining (the process of creating Bitcoin) each day at the current rate. Bitcoin also goes through a halving cycle every four years where the amount of Bitcoin that can be mined each day cuts in half. Sometime around 2028, there will only be 225

BTC mined each day. By roughly 2030, it will be 112.5 mined a day, and so on.

Sometime in 2140, the last Bitcoin will be mined, and there will never be another BTC created ever again.

How easily can Bitcoin be transferred?

It can be transferred with your phone, the same way you would send an email. Copy the address of the receiver and press the Send button. (Just make sure you get the address right, because once it's sent, it can't be unsent.) It can be transferred anywhere in the world in minutes, without using a centralized bank.

So which do you consider money now?

Bitcoin has an ultimate limited supply, and the US dollar doesn't.

As the US government prints billions, and creates trillions more in a computer, the dollar will continue to lose its value. The faster they print it, the faster the US dollar will decline in value.

Oh yeah! And let's not forget, "they" are now proposing a central bank digital currency (CBDC). It will be "virtual" and created by computers and make our money fully centralized (and controlled) by big government. They won't even need to run the printing press anymore to "create it." (And just like the current dollar, they won't have any limit on how many they can create. Big improvement, right?)

They will just press buttons and steal your wealth.

 If you buy Bitcoin with a margin loan, you are betting up on Bitcoin and betting down on the dollar!

37

Bitcoin ETFs

The Smart Way to Hold Digital Gold Without the Hassle

> **di·ver·si·fi·ca·tion**
>
> /də͵vərsəfəˈkāSH(ə)n,dī͵vərsəfəˈkāSH(ə)n/
>
> *noun*
>
> an investment strategy based on the premise that a portfolio with different asset types will perform better than one with few

In the last chapter, we covered the fundamentals of Bitcoin, its scarcity, its decentralized nature, why it has become the go-to digital asset for many, and why in many ways it beats toilet paper "money." But for those who like the idea of owning Bitcoin without dealing with private keys, wallets, or the constant worry about exchange security, there's a solution I've been using that's been gaining traction: Bitcoin ETFs.

Now, we've mentioned them before in this book, and you're probably familiar with ETFs (exchange-traded funds). They're baskets of assets that trade on stock exchanges, allowing you to invest in things like tech stocks, bonds, specific markets, or even an entire exchange like the NASDAQ or S&P500, in a single, easy-to-buy share. So when Bitcoin ETFs hit the market, it was a game-changer for people who wanted some Bitcoin without the technical challenges of owning actual Bitcoin. Think of it like buying gold without the hassle of having to lug gold bars around in your pocket.

But how do Bitcoin ETFs fit into our broader wealth-building and tax-avoidance strategy—specifically, the Buy, Borrow, Die method that we've been talking about this whole book? Let's get into it.

A BRIEF HISTORY OF BITCOIN ETFs: THE ROAD TO APPROVAL

For years, investors and financial institutions were begging for Bitcoin ETFs. But due to regulatory hurdles (you mean the government doesn't work quickly? I'm shocked!), these products took a while to get the green light. The US Securities and Exchange Commission (SEC) wasn't rushing to approve them because, let's face it, Bitcoin was still viewed as the Wild West of the financial world. Concerns about volatility, fraud, and market manipulation delayed the arrival of these funds.

October 2021 was when the first futures-based Bitcoin ETF—the ProShares Bitcoin Strategy ETF (BITO)—was approved by the SEC. While this was a big step forward, futures-based ETFs don't hold actual Bitcoin. Instead, they track the price of Bitcoin via futures contracts, which, for most investors, wasn't the pure exposure they were looking for. After all, if you believe in Bitcoin's long-term potential (and if you're buying it as part of Buy, Borrow, Die, the long-term potential is what you should be concerned with), wouldn't you want to own the real thing—or at least an ETF that holds it?

The wait finally ended in January 2024 (which was surprisingly fast for a government agency) when the SEC approved the first spot-traded Bitcoin ETF (meaning the fund holds Bitcoin). This was the breakthrough a lot of folks had been waiting for, myself included, and it made owning Bitcoin as easy as buying shares of stock.

WHY BITCOIN ETFs?

You're probably wondering, "But Mark, why bother with a Bitcoin ETF when I can just buy Bitcoin directly through platforms like Coinbase or Robinhood?"

Good question. While buying actual Bitcoin has its perks (like being able to store it in your own private wallet and to spend and transfer it directly without having to go through an exchange), ETFs come with a few notable advantages:

- **Simplicity.** No need to worry about private keys, digital wallets, or the risk of losing your Bitcoin if you forget a password. With a Bitcoin ETF, you're buying a product you already know—an ETF that trades just like a stock.
- **Security.** Bitcoin ETFs are typically insured and overseen by major financial institutions, which adds a layer of security. When you hold Bitcoin on an exchange, there's a risk of that exchange going bankrupt (I mean, just look at what recently happened with FTX) or being hacked. But a Bitcoin ETF, especially one

regulated in the US, is protected by SIPC insurance, which covers up to $500,000 in case of brokerage failure.

- **Liquidity.** ETFs are easy to trade. You can buy and sell shares just like you would with a stock. No need to worry about exchange downtime or withdrawal limits. Heck, you can even buy and sell them on your phone with your M1 or Robinhood account.

BUY, BORROW, DIE: THE BITCOIN ETF EDITION

Let's dive into the exciting part—how Bitcoin ETFs fit seamlessly into the Buy, Borrow, Die strategy. If you ask me, this is where it gets exciting.

Bitcoin ETFs aren't just a way to invest in the future of money—they're a tool for creating tax-free wealth, borrowing without selling, and building a financial legacy that lasts generations. Sound intriguing? Let's break it down.

Step 1: Buy

The first step is simple—buy Bitcoin ETFs. Instead of navigating the complex world of digital wallets and private keys, you can scoop up shares of a Bitcoin ETF through your brokerage account, Roth IRA (meh), or (shudder, gag) IRA. The ETF's value moves with the price of Bitcoin, so you're getting exposure to Bitcoin's upside without the hassles of owning it directly.

Step 2: Borrow

Now, here's where the magic happens. Instead of selling your Bitcoin ETF when you need cash and triggering capital gains taxes, just like the rest of your investment portfolio, you borrow against your Bitcoin ETF holdings using margin loans.

Why is this important? Remember, when you sell, you trigger a taxable event; and depending on how much Bitcoin has surged in value (and Bitcoin can surge in value), that could mean handing over a significant chunk of your gains to Uncle Sam. By borrowing against your ETFs, you get access to cash without selling the asset and without triggering capital gains taxes.

So how does this work in practice? Let's say Bitcoin goes on one of its famous rallies, and your Bitcoin ETF skyrockets in value. Instead of cashing out, you borrow against your holdings at a low-interest rate. The best part? That loan isn't taxed because, technically, it's not income. It's just a loan you can use for whatever you want—more investments, diversification into other ETFs, or purchase of some real estate for more tax avoidance.

Step 3: Die

All right, this is the part no one likes to think about—but it's a crucial piece of the strategy. When you pass away, just like with your regular ETFs, your heirs inherit your Bitcoin ETFs with a stepped-up basis. This means they won't owe any taxes on the appreciation that occurred during your lifetime. It's like a reset button for capital gains taxes (that we're already avoiding anyway by never selling), making this a tax-efficient way to pass on wealth.

WHY HOLD BITCOIN ETFs
IN A RETIREMENT ACCOUNT?

Let's touch briefly on this: Yes, you can hold Bitcoin ETFs in a retirement account, like an IRA (cue the gag reflex!) or Roth IRA. And I know I'm beating a dead horse at this point, but just a reminder—it's not the best strategy (it's not even a good strategy) to hold them in an IRA if you're planning to use the Buy, Borrow, Die strategy. Why? Because money (and assets) in a retirement account is DEAD MONEY; i.e., you can't borrow secured by the assets. Granted, a Roth IRA doesn't have the tax issues of a traditional IRA, so you could use it to diversify your holdings and eventually sell your ETFs for liquidity—but doing so means killing the golden goose (selling off your assets) just to access the eggs (the future growth in value) she's laying for you.

Do yourself a favor, and if you decide you want Bitcoin ETFs as part of your portfolio, buy them in a taxable brokerage account where you can fully leverage the borrowing strategy. Trust me, your future self—and your wallet—will thank you.

USING BITCOIN ETFs AS PART
OF A DIVERSIFIED STRATEGY

At this point, you might be thinking, "Okay, I get it—Bitcoin ETFs are cool. But how do they fit into my broader portfolio?" The great thing about Bitcoin ETFs is that they can complement other asset classes like stocks, precious metals, and real estate. While Bitcoin's correlation to traditional markets has varied over time, it often behaves differently than stocks or bonds, which can add a layer of diversification to your portfolio.

Additionally, during periods of rising inflation, Bitcoin is sometimes viewed as a safe haven for investors. With Bitcoin ETFs, you can now easily add that layer of protection to your portfolio without diving headfirst into the deep end of the cryptocurrency pool.

BUY, BORROW, HODL

Bitcoin ETFs bring the best of both worlds: exposure to Bitcoin's explosive potential and the simplicity of a regulated, insured financial product. And when you pair them with Buy, Borrow, Die, you're setting yourself up for long-term wealth accumulation while paying (say it with me, folks) ZERO TAXES!

Personally, I'm always adding more Bitcoin ETFs to my portfolio. I'll never sell them, and why would I? I'll just borrow against them when I need cash, let them appreciate over time, and pass them on to my heirs—tax-free.

So the next time you're looking to diversify, grow your wealth, and outsmart Uncle Sam, consider adding Bitcoin ETFs to your portfolio. Keep buying, hold on tight, and never sell—and when Bitcoin reaches its next all-time high, you'll be glad you did.

Almost 95% of the Bitcoin is already mined, leaving the world to compete for the remaining 5%.

Think "supply vs demand" and "risk vs reward."

PART FIVE

Precious Metals

*The Fifth Pillar of a
Buy, Borrow, Die Strategy*

The Five Pillars

38

Golden Opportunities

*Leveraging Buy, Borrow, Die to Acquire
Gold and Precious Metals*

> **pre·cious met·als**
>
> /ˈpreSHəs ˈmedlz/
>
> *noun*
>
> rare, naturally occurring metallic chemical elements of
> high economic value; gold, silver, platinum

So you're intrigued by the glitter of gold—who wouldn't be? For thousands of years, people have been drawn to shiny things that hold their value, and gold has always been at the top of the list. But what if I told you there's a way to borrow against your assets to buy gold, then borrow against your gold to buy even more assets—and keep repeating the process? All this without ever selling anything and even building a system where, in the future, you could live off the (tax-free) money you borrow? It's the wealth-building cycle of buying and borrowing—and today we're taking that strategy and applying it to the world of gold, precious metals, and smart borrowing.

Let's break it down.

WHY GOLD (AND PRECIOUS METALS)?

Gold and other precious metals have long been a reliable store of value—whether the economy is booming or crumbling like a poorly made soufflé (does anyone even cook soufflés anymore?), precious metals remain steady. They act as a noncorrelated hedge against market volatility. When your stock portfolio is on a roller coaster, gold tends to stay calm. So if you're looking for a way to diversify, preserve wealth, and avoid sleepless nights, gold (and other precious metals) can be a solid bet.

Now, here's the intriguing part—you can acquire gold without selling off your existing investments. By borrowing against your assets, you can buy gold, then borrow against that gold to acquire even more assets, and keep repeating the process—all while paying little to no taxes.

Step 1: Buy (But Not with Your Own Money)

Here's where the magic of Buy, Borrow, Die kicks in. You already know you can use other people's money (OPM) to build wealth. One of the best ways to do this is by borrowing against your existing assets. Let's say you have a healthy portfolio of stocks and/or real estate. Why sell those assets and trigger a taxable event when you can simply take a loan against them?

Margin loans allow you to borrow against your portfolio at low-interest rates, and since you're not selling anything, you won't trigger capital gains taxes. Congratulations—you've now got tax-free money! You didn't work for it, you didn't pay taxes on it, and now, you can use it to buy gold or other precious metals. But don't stop there—this is just the beginning of the wealth-building cycle.

Step 2: Borrow Against Your Gold

Now that you own gold, it's time to level up. Services like TDS Vaults, CFC, and JM Bullion allow you to safely store your precious metals while offering an additional benefit—you can borrow against those metals. You see where I'm going with this, right? You bought the gold using borrowed funds, and now you can borrow against the value of that gold, effectively doubling your leverage.

With these services, your gold sits safely in a vault, and you can take out loans against its value without ever selling it. This means you can use the borrowed money to buy even more gold (or other assets). The cycle continues—borrow, buy more, repeat. The best part? You still haven't sold anything, so no capital gains taxes. It's a perpetual cycle of compounding wealth.

Step 3: Protect Yourself from Market Chaos

Gold, silver, and other precious metals act as a hedge against inflation and market instability. When the stock market tanks or inflation eats away at the value of the dollar, gold tends to go up. It's like that one friend who always stays calm when everyone else is panicking. So when the markets are having a bad day (or year), your gold acts as a safety net, ensuring that a portion of your wealth is protected from the chaos.

Plus borrowing against your gold allows you to access liquidity even when the broader economy is struggling. You're essentially insulating yourself from market volatility while continuing to grow your wealth.

Step 4: Die (and Pass It All On, Tax-Free)

I know, this is everyone's least favorite part of the Buy, Borrow, Die strategy. But hear me out—it's where the real tax magic happens. Once you've borrowed against your assets, bought your gold, and borrowed against that gold, the wealth-building cycle keeps spinning. And when it's time to pass your assets on to your heirs, they'll receive them with a step-up in basis, meaning they won't owe any capital gains taxes on the appreciation during your lifetime. They inherit your gold tax-free, and the wealth-building process continues.

It's a win-win.

BONUS: A HEDGE AND A GROWTH ENGINE IN ONE

One of the key reasons that gold makes such a strong addition to this strategy is that it's noncorrelated with traditional assets like stocks, bonds, and ETFs. This means it tends to perform well when other parts of your portfolio aren't. So even when the markets are volatile, your gold will help stabilize your overall wealth.

In summary, combining the Buy, Borrow, Die strategy with gold and precious metals through these services is like unlocking a secret level in the wealth game. You preserve your existing wealth, tap into new investments, and dodge Uncle Sam's tax traps—all while setting yourself (and your heirs) up for long-term financial success.

Who knew buying shiny things could be so strategic?

Consider leveraging your portfolio to buy gold, then borrow against the gold to snag stocks after a crash to supercharge your recovery!

PART SIX

Business Ownership

*The Solid Foundation of a
Buy, Borrow, Die Strategy*

The Five Pillars

39

Tacos, Tequila, and Tax Breaks

Maximizing Your Business Deductions

> **en·tre·pre·neur·ship**
> /ˌäntrəprəˈnər ˌSHip, ˌäntrəprəˈnoŏr ˌSHip/
> *noun*
> the activity of setting up a business or businesses, and taking on financial risks in the hope of profit

Who doesn't love tacos? Now, imagine those tacos coming with a side of tax savings. That's right! When you own a business, even something as simple as a taco can be tax-deductible. Throw in a margarita, and you've got yourself a tax-deductible Tacos and Tequila Tuesday. But before we dive into the delicious details, let's explore why this matters and how it connects to the broader US tax system.

WHAT IS A PROGRESSIVE TAX SYSTEM?

The US operates under a "progressive" tax system. But what does that mean? In simple terms, the more money you make, the higher the percentage of that income you pay in taxes. This is different from a flat tax, where everyone pays the same percentage, no matter how much they earn.

The idea behind a progressive tax system is fairness. Those who earn more have the financial resources to contribute more to public services and infrastructure, while lower-income earners pay a smaller share. In theory, it's designed so that everyone pays their "fair share." But is it working? Well, not entirely.

For the poorest Americans, the system works—they often pay no taxes. But for the average person, many end up overpaying. It's estimated that 20–25% of the 168 million Americans who file taxes will overpay. That's as many as 42 million people paying more than they owe. And here's the kicker: The taxman will always notify you if you underpay your taxes, but they will never notify you if you overpay them. Funny how that works, eh?

SO WHO PAYS AND WHO DOESN'T?

The truth is, those who've taken the time and put in the effort to raise their financial IQ pay little-to-no taxes, regardless of their income. On the other hand, those who aren't as financially savvy end up shouldering most of the tax burden. So how do you become "financially savvy" and avoid being one of those paying more than they need to? One effective strategy is understanding the power of business ownership. (*Hint:* There's a reason why I say that business ownership is the strong, stable base of any effective Buy, Borrow, Die strategy. It empowers so much of what we do, especially on the tax-avoidance and tax-savings side.)

STARTING A BUSINESS: IT IS EASIER THAN YOU THINK!

A common question I hear is, "How do I start a business?"

Starting a business doesn't require forming a corporation—though it can be useful, as we'll discuss—or paying government fees, which are just another tax. It simply requires an idea, a product, or a service to sell, and the intention to make a profit. That's it. Simple, right?

For example, if you bake cookies in your kitchen and sell them to your neighbors, you have a legitimate business. (And if you ever need a taste tester for those cookies, I volunteer.) Or if you launch a YouTube channel sharing the healthiest pet food options and aim to profit—whether through ad revenue or selling the products you recommend—you've just started a business! The key is to produce income—when you do, you can deduct your business expenses, and what's left is your profit.

COMMON BUSINESS DEDUCTIONS

The goal is to identify legitimate business expenses that can be deducted to reduce your taxes. Here are some common deductions:

- **Salaries and wages.** Paying employees, including yourself
- **Rent or mortgage.** If you rent or own space for your business

- **Health insurance.** Premiums paid for yourself and your employees
- **Advertising and marketing.** Costs of promoting your business
- **Depreciation.** Large purchases like computers or equipment, which can be deducted over time. (You can even depreciate any vehicles you buy for your business, but we'll get into that later.)

Even part of your car payment (or mileage) and cell phone usage can be deducted as business expenses. If you're baking cookies, ingredients, bakeware, and even a business-only oven are deductible. If you use a room in your home exclusively for business, you can deduct a portion of your rent or mortgage, utilities, and other expenses.

For that YouTuber discussing the healthiest pet foods, costs related to the pet food or supplies purchased for creating content can also be deducted. Heck, if you're recording the content using your phone, you could deduct part of the cost of your phone too!

As your business grows, you can even deduct the cost of a celebratory dinner on Taco Tuesday as a legitimate business expense. And yes, you can hire your spouse and kids to help run the business. As long as they provide a legitimate service, their wages are deductible.

HIRING YOUR FAMILY

Are you thinking, "Can I really hire my spouse and kids?"

Yes, you can! For example, if your spouse helps with filming, editing, and producing YouTube content, or if your kids appear in videos with your furry pet food reviewers "Snoopy" or "Garfield," they can be paid as actors, and it's a legitimate business expense.

REAL ESTATE: MY FAVORITE BUSINESS OPPORTUNITY

I realize that baking cookies or starting a YouTube channel isn't for everyone. But here's my favorite strategy: buying real estate and renting out a portion of it. Once you rent it, you have a business. If your business operates out of your home, that can add up to even more deductions.

Remember, though, all expenses must be legitimate business expenses. This is where having the right CPA or licensed tax professional is crucial—they help you find and maximize deductions to minimize your taxes.

TEACHING TAX SAVINGS TO YOUR KIDS

Before we move on, here are some great ways to reduce your tax bill while boosting your kids' financial IQ:

- **Hire your kids**. In 2024, you can pay each child up to $13,850 tax-free annually. This is a deduction for you, and it's likely not taxable for them since that amount isn't taxed.
- **Set up a custodial account.** Open a custodial account for your kids, and let them invest their earnings. It teaches them the power of investing and shows them how to grow their wealth tax-free.

- **Teach them the power of borrowing.** While they can't borrow from their account until they're 18, when they do, they can convert it to a regular brokerage account and borrow against their stocks and ETFs. Be sure to ask them:
  - "Did you work for this money?"
  - "Did you pay taxes on it?"
  - "Did you fight inflation while earning it?"

Teach your kids the difference between assets and liabilities. Let them know, "Working hard is highly taxed, but learning how to use debt is tax-free and much easier than working."

Buy, Borrow, Die is about teaching your family how to build multigenerational wealth, and it starts with you. Wealth doesn't buy happiness, but it does buy freedom—from our failing school system, from student loans, and from becoming a slave to the banks.

If you don't educate them, someone else will—starting with, "Go to school, get a job, save money, get good credit, and contribute to a retirement account so you can retire someday."

Ugh, there's that gag reflex again—I need to get that checked out.

School isn't education; it's indoctrination. Check out https://2hourlearning.com for an alternative.

40

S-Corp Secrets

*How to Slash Your Taxes and
Keep More of Your Money*

cor·po·ra·tion

/ ˌkôrpə ˈ rāSHən/

noun

a company or group of people authorized to act as a single
entity (legally a person) and recognized as such in law

I had a Zoom call scheduled with Dave, a new student of The
Perfect Portfolio course; and when he appeared on my computer screen, I noticed he was surrounded with paperwork and
had a confused look on his face. Uh oh.

"Dave, you look like you're about to dive into a sea of paperwork and drown in tax jargon. What's going on?" I asked.

"Mark, these taxes are killing me," Dave said. "I started my
business last year, and now the IRS wants a piece of everything I
make! My accountant mentioned something about an S-Corp,
but I have no idea what that is. Help?"

Oh, this was going to be good. "Ah, the good ol' S-Corp. Let me tell you, Dave, the S-Corp is like the secret weapon in the tax-saving arsenal. But first, I've got to ask—how much are you paying yourself right now from your business?"

Dave laughed nervously. "Well . . . all of it. I mean, I am the business."

"Bingo! That's exactly where you're leaking money to the taxman. Let's take a step back and talk about why the S-Corp could be your new best friend. But I promise I'll make it painless, maybe even fun."

WHAT IS AN S-CORP, AND WHY SHOULD YOU CARE?

First off, contrary to what a lot of folks think, an S-Corp (short for "Subchapter S Corporation") is not a type of business structure. It's a tax status that your business can elect with the IRS. You can keep your business as an LLC or corporation, but you choose to have it taxed like an S-Corp. Why would you want to do that? One simple reason: You get to pay yourself in a much smarter way.

Here's the deal: When you run a business and take all the money home as a salary or a distribution, you're getting smacked with self-employment taxes. (Getting smacked with any taxes is bad, but self-employment taxes are some of the worst. Remember what we said about how it seems like they tax you for the things they don't want you to do? It's almost like they don't want you starting up your own business and being self-reliant.) Those self-employment taxes are nasty, with an extra 15.3% for social security and Medicare. That's on top of your regular income tax. It's like getting taxed to death . . . twice.

Dave visibly gulped and looked like he was going to be sick. "Wait, so I'm paying double?"

"Pretty much. But with an S-Corp, you get to divide your income into two parts—a reasonable salary and distributions. You still pay self-employment taxes on the salary, but here's the beauty of it—those juicy distributions are NOT subject to self-employment taxes."

He obviously liked the sound of that. "You're telling me I can take home money without paying that extra tax?"

"That's right! The IRS only cares that you pay yourself a reasonable salary for the work you do, and the rest can come out as distributions. Less self-employment tax means more tacos for you."

HOW DOES IT ACTUALLY WORK?

Let's make this real with some numbers, shall we?

Say your business pulls in $100,000 this year. If you take it all as salary, you're paying self-employment tax on the entire $100,000. That's around $15,300 in self-employment taxes alone, not even counting income tax.

Now, if you were an S-Corp, you could pay yourself a reasonable salary—let's say $50,000. On that $50,000, you'll pay the same self-employment taxes (about $7,650). But the other $50,000? That's a distribution, and guess what? No self-employment tax on that. You just saved yourself about $7,650. Boom!

I know you're thinking: "Wait, so I could save thousands off my taxes just by splitting how I pay myself? Why don't they teach this stuff in school?"

The answer is simple: Because school wants you to be a worker bee, not a tax-saving ninja. But don't worry, I've got you covered.

THE CATCH: YOU NEED TO PLAY BY THE RULES

Now, before you start doing backflips over all that money you're going to save, there's a catch: The IRS doesn't just let you call 90% of your income a distribution and 10% a salary. You've got to pay yourself a reasonable salary.

What's a reasonable salary? Do I just guess? You wish! The IRS loves being vague about this. Basically, the IRS expects you to pay yourself what you'd have to pay someone else to do the same work. If you're a plumber, what does a plumber in your area make? If you're an accountant, same deal. You can't just pay yourself $10,000 and take the rest as distributions—they'll catch on to that faster than you can say "audit."

S-CORP SETUP: IT'S EASIER THAN YOU THINK

The next question people usually ask me is: "But isn't setting up an S-Corp a nightmare?"

The answer: nope. Here's the step-by-step on how to do it:

1. **Form your business.** First, your business needs to be an LLC or a corporation. You can elect S-Corp status for either one.
2. **File Form 2553.** This is the magic form you send to the IRS to elect S-Corp status. It's short, it's sweet, and you can even have your CPA handle it for you.
3. **Start paying yourself a salary.** Once you're an S-Corp, you'll need to set up payroll and start paying yourself that reasonable salary we talked about. Don't worry; payroll services are a breeze these days with software like Gusto or QuickBooks Payroll.
4. **Take distributions.** Whatever is left after your salary, you can take out as distributions, saving on that self-employment tax.

That doesn't sound too bad, does it? But how much is this going to cost you?

Good question. You'll have some costs—like setting up payroll and potentially working with a CPA—but those pale in comparison to what you could save in taxes. Plus everything you spend to run your S-Corp, like software or bookkeeping services, are tax-deductible business expenses!

WHY THE S-CORP ISN'T FOR EVERYONE (BUT IT MIGHT BE FOR YOU)

The S-Corp isn't a one-size-fits-all solution. If you're making less than $40,000 a year in profit, the savings might not be worth the effort. But once you're pulling in $50,000 or more, the S-Corp could start saving you thousands in taxes every year.

So should you wait until you're making more than $50,000 per year to switch to an S-Corp? Well, I'm not going to tell you what to do, but if your profits are still low, don't rush into it. Once your business hits that sweet spot, though, you're probably going to want to make the switch ASAP. Otherwise, you're just handing money to the IRS that could be sitting in your bank account—or paying for your next vacation.

FINAL THOUGHTS:
SAVE MONEY, BUY TACOS

At the end of the day, avoiding taxes is all about strategy. The S-Corp is just one tool in the toolbox, but it's a powerful one if used right. And the best part? Once you've set it up, you'll be saving money year after year, with less effort than you think.

So are you ready to stop overpaying and start keeping more of what you earn?

Dave now looked a lot happier than when we started the conversation. "Okay, I get it now. I'm in. Let's do this. But first . . . wanna go get some tacos?"

"Now you're speaking my language. And guess what? As an S-Corp owner, that's a tax-deductible business lunch."

If you're planning to write off a meal as a business expense, save the receipt and jot down who you dined with and what you discussed on the back. Think of it as a love note to your CPA—they'll thank you later!

41

Turning Learning into Earning

Making Education a Business Expense

> **de·duct·i·ble**
>
> /də'dəktəb(ə)l/
>
> *adjective*
>
> able to be deducted, especially from taxable income or tax to be paid

Stella and I recently attended the Bitcoin 2024 conference in Nashville. Since I'm writing this book and running a financial education business, the whole trip—hotel, dinners, and, yes, even the tacos—was a legitimate business expense, costing $3,000. The insights we gained were priceless. That $3,000 investment will likely make us millions over time, and by sharing it with you, it could do the same for you. That's exciting!

It's interesting, though—many Americans wouldn't hesitate to drop $3,000 on a lawnmower or sign off on $100,000+ in student loans. But to spend $3,000 to learn about Bitcoin? That makes people pause. I blame it on an education system that teaches how to get a job but doesn't teach how to build and protect wealth.

But here you are. You're investing in your financial education. Kudos! My advice? Never stop learning. It's the best "investment" you'll ever make.

Now, depending on your business—whether you provide a product or service—what counts as a legit education expense can vary. That's why I've diversified my business so almost everything I do is a business expense.

Think about this: I invest in real estate, run a business, and write about tax strategies. Most of my friends are also investors, so when we meet for dinner, it's often business-related, turning tasty meals into tax deductions. And when we attend events like Bitcoin 2024 (or when we go to Bitcoin 2025 next year), that's tax-deductible too. Plus with my YouTube channel, things like computers and TVs become business expenses.

So what's not deductible? While not everything is deductible—you must keep personal and business separate—it's possible to design your social life around business events, and that's exactly what we do. It's enjoyable, and we're constantly learning while growing our passive income streams by buying (and borrowing) to fund our business.

For example: Let's say Stella and I took a $3,000 margin loan for our Bitcoin 2024 trip. That whole trip was a tax-deductible expense, and since the loan wasn't taxed, we got a deduction on money we never paid taxes on. Sounds good, right?

Oh, and since we have a rental property, I'm also planning to buy that $3,000 zero-turn riding lawnmower—another legit expense (and a pretty cool one; it even has cupholders!). If I use a margin loan to buy it, that's another deduction on money I didn't have to earn or pay taxes on. I'll be calculating my tax savings while mowing the lawn.

My advice if you have a job? Start learning and invest heavily in your financial IQ. This means putting in your time and money and hiring a good CPA to handle your taxes. As you make more money and figure out how to create legitimate business expenses, keep learning and focus on lowering that tax bill.

Now, as I've said before, I hated school and dropped out of business school—but what if I told you that since then, I've spent over $100,000 on financial education and advice? What's your first thought? If you're thinking, "I'd never spend $100,000 on education and advice," here's the alternative: You're probably on track to pay millions in taxes and risk ending up broke in your later years, working until the day you die. I know that sounds scary, but it's a harsh reality—and unfortunately, it's the fate awaiting most Americans today.

I've seen it all—poor people become rich, and rich people end up broke. The biggest difference? Who they hang out with and where they get their education.

You become the average of the five people you spend your time with.

Choose wisely.

42

Section 179 Savings

Buy a Tesla for Your Business

> **qual·i·fy·ing**
> /ˈkwôləˌfīiNG, ˈkwäləˌfīiNG/
> *adjective*
> denoting someone or something that is entitled to a
> particular benefit or privilege by fulfilling a necessary
> condition for something

The first time I laid eyes on a Tesla Model S, I was hooked. It was sleek, futuristic, and everything I imagined a car of the future would be. But back then, owning one seemed like a distant dream. I wasn't in a position to buy it, but deep down, I knew that one day I'd be behind the wheel of a Tesla.

I've admired Elon Musk for as long as I can remember. His relentless drive and visionary thinking convinced me that electric cars weren't just a novelty—they were the future. But what really captivated me was watching a modern-day David take on the Goliaths of the auto industry. Over two decades, Elon

253

Musk battled industry titans who threw everything they had to kill the electric car.

I vividly recall how Tesla was teetering on the edge of bankruptcy in 2008 and again in 2013. The company was on the brink of collapse more than once, but each time, Musk found a way to pull through, defying the odds. Fast-forward to today, and Tesla isn't just surviving—it's thriving. Tesla is now the most valuable car company in the world, and the Tesla Model Y has become the best-selling car globally.

Running a small business myself, I understand the challenges of expansion, but what Elon has accomplished is on another level. He's not just running Tesla; he's simultaneously leading SpaceX, The Boring Company, SolarCity, and Neuralink. And as if that weren't enough, he's now tackling government inefficiency with his upcoming work on DOGE (the Department of Government Efficiency), all while championing free speech through his acquisition of X (formerly Twitter). Now, I'm no Elon Musk, but I am also a purpose-driven entrepreneur, and I know if we lose our First Amendment right of free speech, taxes will be the least of our worries!

Now, let's get back to taxes and learn how buying a Tesla can help us avoid them.

UNDERSTANDING SECTION 179

The Section 179 deduction is a provision in the US tax code that allows businesses to deduct the full purchase price of qualifying equipment (including specific vehicles) and software purchased or financed during the tax year. This deduction is intended to encourage businesses to invest in themselves by purchasing necessary equipment. So rather than depreciate a $100,000 vehicle over five years, business owners can take the full $100,000 deduction in the first year they buy the vehicle.

We'll cover year-end tax planning in a later chapter, but here are the basics of Section 179.

For vehicles, the rules are slightly different than when buying other equipment, especially for vehicles with a gross vehicle weight rating (GVWR) over 6,000 pounds. Both the Tesla Model X and the Cybertruck fall into this category, making them eligible for the largest deduction.

The key benefits of Section 179 for heavy vehicles are as follows:

- **Immediate deduction.** Section 179 allows you to deduct a significant portion—or even the full purchase price— of a qualifying vehicle in the year it is put into service, rather than spreading the depreciation over several years. Keep in mind that the deduction is subject to IRS limits, the vehicle's business use percentage, and other qualifications.
- **Bonus depreciation.** For qualifying vehicles, businesses can also take advantage of bonus depreciation, which allows for an additional deduction after the Section 179 limits are applied.

To qualify for the Section 179 deduction, the Tesla must:

- **Be used for business.** The vehicle must be used for business purposes more than 50% of the time.
- **Be purchased and put into service.** The vehicle must be purchased (not leased) and placed into service within the tax year you are claiming the deduction.

- **Have a GVWR over 6,000 pounds.** The vehicle must meet the weight requirement, which both the Tesla Model X and the Cybertruck do.

CALCULATING THE DEDUCTION

Let's break down the potential tax benefits using a hypothetical scenario:

Suppose you purchase a Tesla Model X for $100,000.

- **Section 179 deduction.** In 2024, you can deduct up to $30,500 of the vehicle's purchase price in the first year (subject to the limits of Section 179).
- **Bonus depreciation.** For the remaining amount ($100,000 – $30,500 = $69,500), you can apply bonus depreciation of up to 60% of the total vehicle price in 2024, allowing you to deduct another $60,000.

Imagine this: You're meeting with your CPA at the end of the year, and your taxable income is sitting at $100,000 after all other deductions. You decide your business needs a truck, so you're going to buy that fully loaded Cybertruck for your business, putting down $10,000. How do you do it? You press the Borrow button on your investment account, take out a loan to cover that $10,000 down payment, finance the remaining $90,000, and with a little tax alchemy under Section 179, your tax bill practically vanishes. Magic, right?

Once again, to take advantage of these deductions, ensure that you maintain proper documentation and speak with your CPA to make sure that you meet all the qualifications and that the tax codes have not changed.

Depending on your location, you may also be eligible for state and local incentives or rebates for purchasing an electric vehicle, further enhancing the tax savings since many of these are tax credits, aka tax-free money back in your pocket!

Also, investigate the perks of adding solar panels to your rental property. You'll save on energy, charge your Tesla, and—wait for it—double dip on tax savings!

Now, I know what you are thinking: "If I buy a Tesla on a Tuesday and grab tacos, does that make it a Tax-Deductible Tacos and Tequila Tuesday in a Tesla?"

Yes, it does (see Figure 42-1).

FIGURE 42-1   Tax-deductible Tacos and Tequila Tuesday in a Tesla. It's a thing. (Just remember not to drink and drive. Don't worry, though; if you need a ride back home after your business taco lunch, the Uber ride is a tax-deductible business expense.)

Year-end tax planning is vital!

43

Tax-Savvy Health

How to Save on Taxes While Protecting Your Well-Being

> **pre·mi·um**
>
> /ˈprēmēəm/
>
> *noun*
>
> an amount to be paid for an insurance policy

S o while this book is all about how ordinary, everyday Americans can legally pay no taxes, let's pause for a moment. Making money is great, but is it really the end goal?

What matters more is what you do with that money. It's like juggling the four Fs: faith, finances, fitness, and family. Have you ever noticed how some people lose their health while building their wealth, only to end up spending their wealth trying to regain their health? I think Zig Ziglar said it best: "Money isn't everything, but it ranks up there with oxygen." And he's right—money is crucial, but it's about finding the right balance.

Now, let's talk about one of the big headaches (no pun intended, considering this is a chapter about health) for all small business owners: health insurance. I've had my share of health issues, and when it comes to picking the right insurance plan? Well, I enjoy it about as much as I enjoy going to the dentist. Maybe even less. Deciding between a plan with a low deductible and high premium or one with a high deductible and low premium is like never having your cake and never eating it too.

As a small business owner, health insurance premiums can be a huge expense. For me, it's about $900 a month! But here's a silver lining: I can deduct 100% of those premiums on my taxes, which makes it hurt a little less. Knowing how to deduct these costs can really help lower your taxable income.

Here's the scoop on health insurance premiums:

- If you're self-employed and don't have another health plan, you can deduct 100% of your health insurance premiums. This deduction reduces your adjusted gross income (AGI), and you can still take it even if you don't itemize deductions.
- Of course, you need to have a net profit for the year, and the deduction can't exceed your net profit.

What if you're an S Corporation owner?

- If you own more than 2% of an S Corporation, the corporation can pay your health insurance premiums. These premiums are included in your wages and are subject to income tax but not social security and Medicare taxes—if you report them correctly. Then you can deduct these premiums on your personal tax return. Yet another reason why I love S-Corps.

And what about medical expenses?

- Medical expenses are deductible if they exceed 7.5% of your AGI. This includes insurance premiums, dental and vision care, prescription meds, and treatments.

HOW ABOUT HEALTH
SAVINGS ACCOUNTS (HSAs)?

Great question. An HSA is like a tax triple threat: Contributions are tax-deductible, the earnings grow tax-free, and withdrawals are tax-free when used for qualified medical expenses. But remember, you must have a high-deductible health plan (HDHP) to contribute.

So by understanding how to deduct health insurance premiums and medical expenses, you can reduce your taxable income, keep more money in your pocket, and invest in your health in a tax-advantaged way too. Learn the rules, keep good records, and you'll manage your healthcare costs more effectively.

Consider a Health Savings Account—it's triple tax-free!

44

Year-End Tax Planning

Bigger Savings in the Final Stretch

> **tax plan·ning**
> /ˈtaks planiNG/
> *noun*
> the process of analyzing a person's financial situation and making use of tax laws to pay the least amount of taxes possible

I t doesn't matter if you are a new investor starting with $100 or a sophisticated investor that owns a business and real estate. Either way, year-end tax planning is a must, and missing an IRS deadline can be an expensive mistake and could result in both penalties and interest. But by being proactive throughout the year, you can avoid the tax bill in the first place—and "penalties and interest" can't be applied on a refund.

Your tax planning should start in January and end in December, and yes, finding a great CPA is a must.

So how do you find a great CPA?

Apply the same principle to finding a great CPA as when visiting a great restaurant. If you get incredible service, go back again and pay a little extra.

Have you even been to a great restaurant and given an extra-large tip, and the next time you go, a complimentary dessert or drink has been served? The same applies to a CPA when you find one: Be sure to pay them very well and you'll get better service, and likely a lower tax bill.

But I will admit, it is much easier to find a great server at a restaurant than it is to find a great CPA.

Here is the secret: Learn all the tax codes that you want to use to reduce your tax bill, meet with a few CPAs, and let them know, "I want to implement all these tax codes, and eventually I want to pay little-to-no taxes. Can you help?"

Ask them what they charge and how much they estimate you will save in taxes. If the tax savings is much larger than the bill, pay the bill, plus a little extra, and buy your CPA dinner to say thank you. (And be sure to tip your server at the restaurant appropriately if they provide great service!)

Just imagine if you were a CPA, what level of service would you provide to a customer who treated you like that?

In The Perfect Portfolio course, we identified some specific dates to add to your planner to simplify your tax planning, and I want to share them with you too. Remember, tax planning isn't just about filing forms—it's about being strategic. By planning early and reviewing your progress throughout the year, you'll find plenty of opportunities to reduce your tax liability and grow your wealth, so start planning now and check in with your CPA regularly. And don't forget—use the tools available to you: paying your kids and funding their custodial accounts, borrowing from your brokerage account to fund your IUL (your tax-free family bank), and borrowing again to fund charitable contributions. This is a powerful strategy since donating is a tax deduction, but donating using borrowed funds through a margin loan creates a double tax deduction—you're deducting money that has never been taxed! These strategies can save you a ton in taxes—but only if you plan ahead.

SPECIFIC DATES FOR YOUR YEAR-END TAX PLANNER

To help simplify your tax planning, here are some important dates to mark on your calendar, straight from The Perfect Portfolio course:

February 1st: Write Down Your Goals and Start Tax Planning

- This is the day to set the tone for your financial year. Write down your goals, including asset purchases, tax planning, and passive income objectives.
- Consider funding your "tax-free family bank" and exploring the strategic purchases you can make during the year using loans from your policy. Your policy can serve as additional emergency reserves, provide a down payment for real estate, or fund other investments. Remember, the purpose of your IUL is uniquely tailored to your goals, and those goals may evolve from year to year. Keep it flexible and aligned with your financial priorities.
- Set up custodial accounts: Fund your kids' futures by giving them jobs that bring real value to your company,

and deposit their pay into their M1 Custodial Accounts. Pay them the maximum allowed by the IRS—just make sure it's a legitimate role!

- Consider whether you plan to purchase any real estate and take into account the significant tax advantages these investments can offer. Remember, real estate is one of the most powerful tools for legally reducing your tax bill, and strategic purchases can help offset taxes for many years to come.

March 15th: S-Corp and Partnership Tax Return Deadline

- This is your deadline for filing tax returns if you have an S-Corp or partnership. Make sure to file an extension, if necessary, but don't miss this date.

April 15th: Individual Tax Return Deadline

- The big one! Individual tax returns are due, along with any outstanding payments. This is also your last chance to make contributions to IRAs (hopefully Roth IRAs and not *gag* the other ones) and HSAs for the prior tax year. If you're self-employed, this is the first estimated tax payment deadline as well.

May 1st: Review Your Progress

- By now, it's time to review how you're doing with the goals you set in February. Are you making progress on your asset purchases and passive income goals? Assess your progress and make adjustments as necessary.

June 15th: Second-Quarter Estimated Payments

- For those who pay estimated taxes, the second-quarter payment is due. Keep ahead of these payments to avoid penalties and interest.

August 1st: Prepare for "Sell September"

- "Sell September" is a common market trend, where we often see a pullback in stocks. Ask yourself, "How much cash or liquid reserves do I have in case of a downturn?" This is the perfect time to start preparing your portfolio for volatility.

September 15th: Third-Quarter Estimated Payments

- Third-quarter estimated taxes are due. Again, staying on top of these quarterly payments helps avoid nasty surprises come tax time.

October 15th: Final Extension Deadline

- If you filed for an extension back in April, this is your last chance to get that tax return in. Miss this deadline, and penalties start stacking up.

November 1st: Review Year-End Tax-Loss Harvesting

- Time to check in on possible tax-loss harvesting opportunities within your investment portfolio. If some of your investments have lost value since you purchased them, consider selling to offset capital gains.
- Make annual donations: If you're planning to make charitable contributions, now's the perfect time to act. Consider pressing that Borrow button to maximize those "double tax deductions."
- Consider vehicle purchases: Need a new vehicle? Consider purchasing one over 6,000 pounds to take advantage of additional tax deductions. (Remember Chapter 42?)
- Meet with your CPA: Map out your final year-end tax-saving moves. And remember . . . what is your goal? The same goal it is every year . . . **to reduce your tax bill to ZERO!**

December 31st: Final Tax-Saving Moves

- This is the last day to implement any tax-saving strategies for the year. Finalize any charitable contributions and make any significant equipment or vehicle purchases for your business.

WRAPPING UP: A YEAR-ROUND STRATEGY

Tax planning isn't something you want to leave until the last minute—just like you wouldn't wait until Christmas Eve to buy your holiday gifts (though I know some people who try. I swear I'm not one of them—really). The earlier you plan, the more opportunities you'll find to reduce your tax bill and keep more of your hard-earned money.

So the idea is to plan early, find a CPA who knows their stuff (hopefully, one who understands "Buy, Borrow, Die"), and follow through on these dates. Think of it like prepping for a marathon. You don't wait until the last mile to start training, right? By getting ahead of the deadlines and working with a smart CPA, you're setting yourself up for bigger savings and fewer headaches.

Review your goals and tax strategies regularly throughout the year, and by December 31st, you'll keep more of what you've earned.

PART SEVEN

Advanced Concepts

*Improving the Performance of a
Buy, Borrow, Die Strategy*

The Five Pillars

45

Rollover Danger

Why Great Returns May Not Be Great for You

roll·o·ver

/ˈrōlˌōvər/

noun

the extension or transfer of a debt or other financial

arrangement

"Hey, Babe. What should I do with my 401(k)?"

This simple question kicked off a conversation between Stella and I when she left her job, leaving behind an old 401(k). As we started planning what to do with it, we knew that the traditional advice from a financial planner would be, "Roll it over to an IRA" (there's my gag response again) or "Transfer it into your new 401(k) at your new employer." Would it surprise you that I wouldn't give the same advice? I certainly hope it's not too big a surprise if you've gotten this far in the book.

I told Stella we wanted to keep her 401(k) working hard for us, growing it aggressively. But doing so inside a traditional IRA just means a bigger slice of our pie goes to Uncle Sam when we eventually want to access it. Instead, our plan was to grow it aggressively with no taxes and convert it to an account where we could use other people's money (OPM) to pay the taxes. Now, I can already hear financial advisors shaking their heads, saying, "That's impossible."

But here's the truth. What amazes me is that the so-called financial advisors suggest investments where you only "win" if you get poor returns. If you get better-than-average returns, it's worse for you and better for the government. Does that really sound like good financial advice?

Let me prove it to you. This truth applies to all tax-deferred retirement accounts.

Imagine someone saves $500 a month in an IRA and earns a 6% average return over 30 years. They'd end up with about $504,000. Because it's tax-deferred (which means that you pay income taxes on your withdrawals, and remember: income taxes are the highest form of all taxation), the government gets to take a good size bite out of that $504,000. But what happens if that diligent investor earns a 12% return over those 30 years?

Well, they're "rewarded" with an account balance of $1,764,000, and now the government gets to take larger bites out of their pie, and even larger bites for the rest of their life, especially if they earn higher-than-average returns. So which would you prefer? A larger account where you owe more taxes, or a smaller account where you owe less?

If financial advisors were truly honest, they'd tell you something like this:

"A tax-deferred account like a 401(k) or IRA only works in your favor if you get poor returns. If you earn better-than-average returns, the bigger the tax bill will be on the back end—especially since these accounts defer income taxes. And the more you grow it, the more likely your distributions will trigger taxation on your social security benefits, which is really just double taxation. So I'll set you up with an IRA and earn you poor returns, so you won't be at risk of double taxation. Sound good?"

This is when financial advisors will say, "But a Roth IRA is a tax-free account." And while that's true, it only further proves my point after they also recommended the tax-deferred retirement account.

A Roth IRA with $1,764,000 is much better than a Roth IRA with $504,000, right? This also means that a Roth IRA is more effective with a higher return and less effective with a lower return, which is the opposite of a traditional IRA or 401(k). The evidence is clear: An IRA or 401(k) only works in your favor with poor returns, but it becomes a tax nightmare if you earn a higher rate of return.

So once again, I conclude that an IRA is only effective for those who are okay with mediocre returns on their retirement account. Is that you?

What if I told you I've got a better alternative? We used it to supercharge our growth and tax efficiency, and we will never use any retirement accounts in the future.

Since we're self-employed, our solution was to open a "Solo" 401(k), also known as an "individual" 401(k), and roll the money into that Solo 401(k). Like any 401(k), you can take a loan from the plan. Stella took a loan, and we invested it in a taxable brokerage account, where it continues to grow completely tax-free, because we will never sell it.

Did you catch that? If we grew her money inside any type of 401(k), our tax bill would get larger as we grew it. But if we grow it in a brokerage account, it will never be taxed if we don't sell it. (Hmm, where have we heard that before?)

Sure, there's interest on the loan, but that's paid back to her if/when she pays back the loan, and it's small compared with the taxes that would be due on the back end.

We also had a plan to stop deferring our taxes. Over the next two years, we liquidated the 401(k) entirely and moved the money into her brokerage account. We've been growing it aggressively, tax-free, and plan to continue doing so for the rest of our lives. And how do we plan to pay any taxes due? Simple. We'll just press the Borrow button and pay whatever taxes are owed. I'd rather pay a tax bill from tax-free growth using money we didn't have to work for or pay taxes on. And now, we're finally free from that horrible tax-deferred retirement account!

Convert your IRA or 401(k) when it's smart—like when a big deduction can offset the taxes.

46

Finding a Fiduciary

Who Wants to Play Where's Waldo?

> **fi·du·ci·ar·y**
> /fəˈdo͞oSHēˌerē,fəˈdo͞osēˌerē/
> *noun*
> a person who holds a legal or ethical relationship of trust
> with one or more other parties

According to the Consumer Financial Protection Bureau:

A fiduciary is someone who manages money or
property for someone else. When you're named a
fiduciary and accept the role, you must—by law—
manage the person's money and property for their
benefit, not yours.

So with that definition in mind, is your financial advisor
really a fiduciary?

Finding a true fiduciary in the world of financial advising can feel like trying to spot Waldo in a crowd of look-alikes. The challenge gets even trickier because many financial advisors work for publicly traded companies. And guess what? Their first fiduciary responsibility isn't to you—it's to their shareholders. Yep, by law, they must focus on maximizing profits for shareholders, not necessarily for you.

This conflict of interest makes it tough for advisors at these firms to truly act in your best interest, no matter how much they say, "I'm a fiduciary financial advisor!"

Remember, fiduciaries have a legal and ethical duty to put your needs first. In financial advising, that means they should prioritize your interests, give you unbiased advice, avoid conflicts of interest, and be transparent in all their dealings.

But here's the kicker: Many financial advisors work for big companies that have one primary goal—boost shareholder value. And that often clashes with the fiduciary responsibility to you, the client.

I wasn't a fiduciary when I first entered the industry, but I was ethical—thanks to my parents for that! I always tried to do what I thought was best for my clients, but here's the catch: What I thought was "best" was just what I was told was best by my supervisors.

After spending years as a fiduciary, I started noticing a pattern. My supervisors only "educated" us on strategies that seemed to benefit shareholders the most. Funny thing, though—I was never invited to those board of directors meetings where they probably mapped out how to maximize profitability for the shareholders. Who knows what really went down in those rooms?

AT THE BEGINNING

When I first learned about the importance of becoming a fiduciary, I got my Series 65 license as fast as I could. Wow, I was finally a fiduciary! I didn't even know that was something I wanted to be when I grew up, but here I was, and I'd made it.

Being a fiduciary investment advisor representative (IAR) came with perks. I could set up accounts without those up-front sales charges I used to have to tack on, and I felt like I was helping my clients in the best way possible.

I started adding more clients to my "book of business" (as they call it). I'd help my clients analyze their assets, liabilities, and cash flow, and give them advice on which accounts were best for them—whether it was investing in a mutual fund or a Roth IRA or making sure they were contributing to their 401(k) to get that sweet employer match. As their account balances grew, so did my income. It was a win-win for everyone!

But after a while, I started to see conflicts everywhere. The biggest red flag? When the founder of the company told us all to only sell one company's products—and surprise, surprise, that company was owned by our parent company. At that moment, I knew I'd be resigning as a "fiduciary."

In 2018, I finally resigned and found myself on a new path—one without the weight of fiduciary responsibility to shareholders hanging over me. It felt like stepping into a whole new world where I could truly focus on what mattered most: helping my clients, not padding a company's bottom line.

Soon after, some friends and I launched a consulting company to provide tax consulting services to real estate and mortgage companies. Our goal? To educate them on the simple yet powerful tax codes that help people legally avoid taxes. We called it REMii Group, which stands for Real Estate, Mortgages, Insurance, and Investing.

Fast-forward five years, and here we are today. I've finally found the formula for paying no taxes. But I couldn't have done it without the adversity along the way and all the experience I gained as a financial advisor. Priceless! I wouldn't change a thing.

Today, I still know a few fiduciary advisors who don't work for publicly traded companies. Most of them are genuinely passionate about their work. They believe their clients would be lost without them, and for many people, their financial advisor is the reason they'll retire comfortably one day.

I've crunched the numbers, and here's the reality: Most Americans will be forced to work until they die because they rely on financial advisors who only sell them retirement accounts. My biggest concern? Their financial advisors might be stuck working forever too. Many don't realize it's possible to pay no taxes, and even if they learned the strategies, they wouldn't be allowed to teach them to you.

In conclusion, finding a real fiduciary financial advisor is tough, especially when most work for big, publicly traded companies. These companies often have hidden conflicts of interest, making it nearly impossible for advisors to put your interests first.

So, what's the solution? Take control by learning the strategies yourself. You might discover you don't "need" a financial advisor after all. Think of it like finding Waldo—it takes some effort, but with the right tools, you'll get there!

No one cares more about your money than you.
Become the best "fiduciary" for your family.

47

Leveraging Correlation

*Amplify Returns with the Buy,
Borrow, Die Strategy*

cor·re·la·tion

/ ˌkôrə ˈlāSHən/

noun

a measure of the relationship between the returns of two
or more assets or investments

I nvesting is like sailing across a wild, unpredictable ocean. The
first rule? Don't let your boat sink—and definitely don't forget
your life raft or life jackets!

To steer your financial ship in the right direction, you need
to understand what drives the markets. One of the most important concepts is correlation. Knowing how different assets move
in relation to each other can mean the difference between your
portfolio staying afloat and going under when the markets get
rough.

So, what exactly is correlation?

In simple terms, correlation is how two assets move in relation to each other. If two assets are positively correlated, they tend to move in the same direction. So if one of your investments goes up by 10% and all your other assets follow suit, they're positively correlated. On the flip side, if they're negatively correlated, one goes up while the other goes down.

Understanding this can help you balance your portfolio, reduce risk, and boost returns. For example, if Portfolio A rises 10% and Portfolio B drops 10%, you could sell some of A and buy more of B. Sounds logical, right? Now, imagine this happening over and over—you sell high and buy low, growing both assets over time. That makes sense, right?

Let's assume that the portfolios did the same thing again: One went up 10%, and one went down. You would do the same, and you would "buy low and sell high" and accumulate more of each asset. The strategy makes sense, but what I don't like about this strategy is the word "sell." If you've ever been told that four-letter words are bad, I agree.

Remember, selling only makes sense when you want to take a loss and Uncle Sam will give you a pat on the back in the form of a tax deduction—aka tax-loss harvesting. But selling when your asset grows? That just triggers taxes, and Uncle Sam doesn't even buy you dinner first.

This is a book about buying and borrowing—our favorite duo. Selling? That's what we save for when we die or when we're tax-loss harvesting! So let's step up the game with negatively correlated assets. That way, we're playing the long game—no selling required.

So let's improve the strategy with assets that are negatively correlated.

If portfolio A goes up by 10% and portfolio B goes down by 10%, it may make sense to take a loan secured by portfolio A, which went up, and buy more of portfolio B, which is now cheaper. If the opposite happened next month, you would do the same, but in reverse: You would borrow from the portfolio that went up by 10% and buy more (10%) of the portfolio that is now cheaper.

If this happened over and over, and you kept borrowing and buying, your portfolio would grow in value, even if the market didn't go up in value. You would continue to own more shares. You would be buying them at cheaper prices and buying them with money you never had to work for that has also never been taxed.

So here's the ultimate plan: Find two assets that are perfectly negatively correlated, moving 10% in opposite directions every month; keep buying and borrowing; and voilà—you'll be rich! Simple, right? (lol)

Now, if you happen to find those magical assets, please do me a favor and let me know so I can jump in too! But until then, let's get back to reality.

Finding noncorrelated assets? Easy. But building a system to take full advantage of each asset's movements while buying and borrowing? That's where things get tricky. Trust me, I didn't even know this strategy had a name until we spent over three years working on it, which eventually led me to write this book and try to simplify it for you.

So let's break down The Five Pillars we use for buying—and borrowing from—to buy more assets:

1. **Stocks and ETFs.** These can move differently from each other, and sometimes they're even negatively correlated. Nice!
2. **Real estate.** Here's the kicker—it also gains value as the dollar weakens. Plus inflation can make your debt "disappear" because it's based on US dollars.
3. **Life insurance.** This one doesn't correlate to the market at all. It only goes up with the market and never down—what's not to love?
4. **Cryptocurrency (Bitcoin and Bitcoin ETFs).** Another asset that benefits when the dollar takes a hit.
5. **Gold and precious metals.** Solid as ever. They rise in value as the US dollar weakens.

Let me explain with an example . . .

Buying real estate with debt can be particularly advantageous in an inflationary environment because the real value of the debt decreases over time, essentially making the debt "disappear."

Let me break it down:

You buy a property for $300,000, putting down just 3%. That means you're taking out a loan for $291,000 at a fixed interest rate of 5% over 30 years. Your monthly payment, including principal, interest, taxes, insurance (and yes, PMI), comes out to about $2,190.

Fast-forward 10 years, with inflation averaging 3% annually. Here's where the magic happens: While the prices of everything else—groceries, gas, and yes, that overpriced coffee you love—keep climbing, your fixed-rate mortgage payment remains locked at $2,190. It doesn't budge.

So, why does the debt seem to "disappear"? Because inflation works in your favor. As wages and prices rise, that $2,190 starts to feel smaller starts feeling like chump change compared with the rising cost of everything else.

In essence, you're paying off your loan with dollars that lose value over time. How cool is that?

Here's how the debt "disappears":

While your mortgage payment remains the same in dollar terms, the real value of those payments decreases because of inflation. In other words, the dollars you use to pay off your mortgage in the future are worth less than they are today. If inflation averages 3% (real inflation is much higher than that) per year, after 10 years, the real value of your monthly payment is significantly lower than when you first took out the loan. If inflation is 4%, your payment is cut in half every 18 years (Rule of 72: 72/18 = 4).

I have more good news when you own real estate. Inflation generally leads to an increase in property values over time. If your property appreciates at the same rate as inflation (or even faster, depending on market conditions), the value of your property will rise while the amount you owe on your mortgage payment remains fixed. This increases your equity in the property, further reducing the real burden of your debt.

If you rent your property, inflation causes rents to rise, and your (tax-free) income can increase and pay down your debt even faster. I'll say it again: Every time I hear someone talk about "paying off debt," all I can think is, "Hello, more taxes!" Because remember, debt is tax-free, but hard work? That's taxed at the highest rate!

As inflation drives up the cost of living, it also tends to increase wages. Over time, your income may rise due to inflation, making your fixed mortgage payments a smaller portion of your overall income. This makes it easier to manage the debt and pay it off, further diminishing its impact. But once again, your goal should be to make less money from "working" and more from tax-advantaged and tax-free income—and compound the growth when buying and borrowing.

Real estate and taxes? They're like opposites. The more real estate you buy (with debt, of course), the less you pay in taxes. Think of it like karate—you want to master the art of tax avoidance. In my best Mr. Miyagi voice: "Real estate on . . . taxes off." (Yes, I'm laughing at my own jokes again—someone's gotta do it, right?)

Back to our example:

Assume after 10 years, due to increasing inflation, the overall value of your property has increased by 40%, and your property is now worth $420,000, and your mortgage balance is only $237,000.

In this scenario, the $291,000 debt you initially took on is now much less significant in real terms because inflation has eroded its value. Note that:

- Your property has appreciated in value, increasing your equity.
- And if you were to *sell* the property, you'd walk away with substantial gains even after paying off the mortgage. (Remember what I said about four-letter words?)

But rather than sell your property, what if you borrowed another 3% ($15,000) from that property as the down payment for a $500,000 home? And yep, once again, you borrow the rest—$485,000 with a 30-year fixed mortgage. Just like before, you're buying a $500,000 property without paying any taxes.

Say it with me: "$500,000 . . . NO TAXES!" You can rent that property in the future, and once again, "Real estate on . . . taxes off!"

Getting the hang of real estate for tax avoidance yet? Did you earn your yellow belt in tax avoidance? Ready to level up to your purple belt and eventually your black belt?

I'll assume you're not done yet, so let's keep sharpening those skills. You ready?

Remember, when you buy real estate with debt, it's like a hedge against the US dollar. Why? Because, like I said earlier:

"Anything with an unlimited supply will go down in value."

And . . .

"Anything with a limited supply will go up in value."

As long as our money isn't backed by anything, can be created endlessly—like printing toilet paper (see Chapter 36)—and exists as digital entries in a computer, its value will inevitably decline, especially when compared to assets with truly limited supply, like real estate.

Real estate will always be in limited supply, and properties in the most desirable neighborhoods? Well, they'll increase in value even faster.

Now, what about gold and precious metals?

Same deal. Gold and precious metals will always go up in value compared with the US dollar, which is on a steady decline.

And what about Bitcoin?

Now, this one's the wild card. Since Bitcoin has a fixed supply of 21 million, and 94.5% of that has already been minted, there's only 5.5% left for the rest of the world to fight over. Basic supply and demand tells us this could get interesting.

Cathie Woods of ARK Invest is predicting Bitcoin at $1 million per BTC by 2030. And Jurrien Timmer (Director of Global Macro) over at Fidelity? He's taking it to the next level, predicting Bitcoin at a whopping $1 billion per BTC by 2038. Yeah, you read that right—$1 billion.

If you're considering jumping on the Bitcoin or Bitcoin ETF train, I highly suggest you check out their full reports. Just search online for ARK Invest's and Fidelity's reports on Bitcoin and cryptocurrency; they're definitely eye-opening (see Figure 48-1).

Okay, now that we have covered the most exciting stuff, like the possibility of a $1 billion BTC price, let's get back to basics and give you some more examples of using correlation, this time when investing in stocks, ETFs and life insurance.

Let's take two ETFs with the same correlation and throw in a basic IUL (indexed universal life insurance), which, as we established earlier, can't lose value even in a market crash. You'll see how these can be supercharged when you combine buying and borrowing.

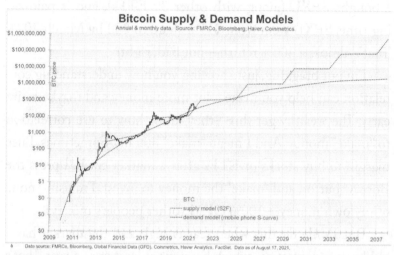

Bitcoin Supply & Demand Models
Annual & monthly data   Source: FMRCo, Bloomberg, Haver, Coinmetrics

Data source: FMRCo, Bloomberg, Global Financial Data (GFD), Coinmetrics, Haver Analytics, FactSet. Data as of August 17, 2021.

FIGURE 48-1   This figure illustrates Bitcoin's supply and demand models as projected up until 2038. It raises the question of whether Bitcoin (BTC) could reach a valuation of $1,000,000 by 2030. For further insights and detailed analysis, refer to the "Fidelity Report: Understanding Bitcoin— What History Will Tell Us" to conduct your own research.

Most investors are familiar with index funds like Vanguard's VOO or State Street's SPY. But I'm guessing not many of you have invested in a 3x ETF like SPXL, which targets 300% of the daily movement of the S&P 500.

Here's the key: SPXL and SPY don't have the same correlation. SPXL amplifies the correlation by 3x.

Now, let's use the COVID crash as an example. (And if you're wondering if I was investing back then, check my Instagram from late April 2020.) The S&P 500 dropped 34%. Scary, right? But I wasn't focused on investing in the S&P 500—I was interested in the S&P X3, which was down about 75%.

So based on what you've learned so far, which one would *you* want to buy?

I knew the stock market would eventually hit a bottom, so I bought SPXL (along with other 3x ETFs), and it paid off big time. SPXL went from $17 a share to $80 by March 2021. That's almost a 400% return—not bad, right?

I'm not bragging, just showing you how understanding correlation can help you make a lot more money and maybe retire early. The wealthy get this—they know how to use correlation to "make" money. And I mean "make" literally. Sometimes, I use margin to buy stocks or ETFs after a market crash. I press the Borrow button and "make" the money to invest. I'm using none of my own money—100% OPM (other people's money).

But I only do this when fear is high and the market has a pullback or correction, which happens at least once a year. That's the perfect time to "make" some money to make more money.

I bet the wheels are turning in your head now. Are you thinking about the possibilities for the next market crash? It's coming—we just don't know when.

Here's where having an IUL is a game-changer. It provides five powerful benefits: life insurance to protect your family, long-term care if you face serious illness, tax-free cash value growth, risk-free returns, and the ability to borrow against the cash value. I don't have an IUL just to "make lots of money"; I have it for all of these benefits—especially the peace of mind that comes from knowing it can't crash. The cash value grows tax-free, and you can access it through loans at any age, for any reason, without applications, credit checks, or strict repayment requirements. That's the real beauty of an IUL: when properly structured and funded, it provides instant, unrestricted access to your money exactly when you need it most.

And when the stock market crashes, well, that's a pretty good reason to borrow. Especially if you understand the power of an index-based ETF like SPXL.

I fund my stocks and ETFs, I borrow each year to fund my IUL, and when the market tanks, I've got plenty of cash that didn't lose value in the crash. I can borrow from my IUL to scoop up stocks and ETFs at a discount.

Now, maybe you don't want to speculate like that while building your Perfect Portfolio. But let me remind you, there's no such thing as "high risk" or "low risk," just risk vs reward. And aiming for an "average rate of return" is for people who don't know how to gauge risk—or how to use other people's money (aka debt) to invest and multiply returns.

Here's something to think about:

Imagine you've been buying index funds in your brokerage account and have $60,000 saved up. You're adding $500 each month to buy more shares. Then you hear about SPXL when it first launches in November 2008. The market's crashing, but you've got a plan.

You think, "I'll take a margin loan and buy $10,000 worth of SPXL and take another loan to buy $500 more every month— while the market keeps tanking."

What do you think it'd be worth today? No peeking.

It'd be worth about $1,860,000. And how much of your own money did you use to buy SPXL?

None. You didn't use any of your money. You didn't have to work for it, and you didn't pay a penny of taxes to create it. Plus you still own your index funds.

You "made" money (tax-free) to make money (tax-free).

Can you see the possibilities of understanding correlation and the power of strategic debt to multiply returns?

One last question: If you didn't use any of your own money to make $1,860,000, what's the rate of return on your money? I'll let you think about that one.

Remember, debt isn't the enemy—taxes are. Borrow smart, invest smarter, and let the market crashes do all the heavy lifting!

48

Live off the Borrow Button

Unlocking Tax-Free Financial Freedom

> **free·dom**
>
> /ˈfrēdəm/
>
> *noun*
>
> the power or right to act, speak, or think as one wants without hindrance or restraint

I magine if my grandparents had been savvy investors during the Great Depression (they weren't, but just imagine that they were). They wouldn't need to be stock market geniuses, just practical. They'd simply have bought shares in the companies whose products they already used daily, investing 10% of their income. Their logic? "We have a telephone, we have a car, we buy gas for the car, and we like having a nice cold Coca-Cola, and we'll always need medical supplies." So they would have invested in AT&T, Ford, Coca-Cola, ExxonMobil, and Johnson & Johnson.

Now, let's have some fun—how much do you think that portfolio would be worth today?

Because of the impact of stock splits, dividends, mergers, and acquisitions, it'd be incredibly hard to calculate exactly, but considering a single share of Coca-Cola purchased when Coca-Cola had its IPO (initial public offering) would be worth over $25 million today, it's safe to say the total value of decades' worth of dollar-cost averaging purchases of those companies would leave you with a portfolio worth hundreds of millions, or even billions, of dollars.

And how would they have done it?

My grandparents would have been "paying themselves first." That means they would have invested before spending on anything else. Week after week, for 4,940 weeks, they would have kept buying more shares, no matter what the market was doing.

Sounds simple, right? Well, the results speak for themselves. If only my grandparents had done this, my life could've been much easier. The stock portfolio would have been passed down to my parents, then to my siblings and me.

But the reality? There's been nothing to inherit in my family, and there hasn't been for generations.

While I didn't inherit anything, but for the purposes of this story, let's pretend I just inherited $3 million of stock! (*Side note:* If anyone wants to leave me $3 million worth of stock in their will, I'd be perfectly okay with that.) Now, I know exactly what I'd do. Do you?

Here's my simple plan: "I'll live off the Borrow button," which means I'd never have to work, and I'd PAY ZERO TAXES. Sounds crazy, right? Just thinking about it is fun.

But let's keep going with this idea . . . and see if the plan holds up.

If I inherited that $3 million, I'd invest it in five companies I use every day. Think about it: We rely on our phone, love driving our Tesla, and AI is part of our daily routine. Heck, I'm even writing this book with Microsoft Word, and don't forget our frequent trips to Home Depot.

So I'd drop $600,000 each into Apple, Tesla, Nvidia, Microsoft, and Home Depot. Simple enough, right?

Let's assume my portfolio grows by an average of 10.5% a year. Using the Rule of 72 (which is simple math), my portfolio would double about every seven years. So in seven years, it would be worth $6 million. Seven years after that, $12 million. Seven years later, $24 million, and so on. And this assumes I never sell a single share.

Crazy, right?

You might be wondering, "If you're never selling your stocks, how will you live?"

I already told you—I'll "live off the Borrow button."

Here's how it works: Instead of selling shares, I'd take out a margin loan each month to cover my expenses. Since loans aren't taxable, I'd get the money tax-free. For example, if I wanted $12,000 a month, I'd borrow that amount and deposit it into my checking account.

Sounds like a sweet deal, right?

This approach saves on taxes in two ways:

1. I'd avoid capital gains taxes by not selling my portfolio.
2. I would be paying no taxes because I wouldn't be earning any income.

Yes, I'd incur some debt and interest, but I'd avoid the bigger tax penalties from selling stocks or earning a salary.

Consider the first month: I borrow $12,000, avoiding the need to earn and pay taxes on a $203,000 annual salary (minus taxes). I'd also avoid capital gains taxes, which would require selling $14,000 worth of stock each month just to net the same $12,000.

Selling stock disrupts future growth, which would otherwise compound tax-free. By simply pressing the Borrow button each month, I'd sidestep the ongoing tax burden and keep my investments growing. Which option sounds better to you?

Here is the best part of the story. If my stock compounded at a 10.5% rate of return, the portfolio would grow to roughly $99 million in 35 years. The only "work" I'd be doing is "pressing the Borrow button" 420 times. Ouch! My finger is tired just thinking about it.

I'm not saying I'll stop working one day and live off the Borrow button. I don't plan to ever "retire." Retirement is a Wall Street concept designed to make people think they must work until they're 65 or 70, pay taxes, and stash money in a retirement account.

I wake up every day with the plan to do what I love. Stella and I both work from home, and we only focus on what we enjoy. I just happen to love teaching people about investing and tax avoidance. By age 90, I could be on book number 27, still teaching others how to build wealth. We also love real estate, so we'll keep buying properties, especially in desirable, low-tax states. Knowing how to maximize the tax benefits makes it even more fun.

I believe anyone can achieve financial independence without waiting until 65 or 70—and without needing a retirement account. Honestly, a simple brokerage account can do the trick, especially if you master the art of buying and borrowing to accumulate more assets.

Doesn't that sound like a better plan than working until you're 70 and getting taxed to death each time you withdraw from your retirement account?

If you're new to investing, start small. Maybe invest $500 a month. Here's an example of how you could diversify:

- Invest $200 a month in two stocks from the "top 10" of the S&P 500—$25 a week in each.
- Invest $200 a month in covered call ETFs—$50 a week.
- Invest $100 a month into Bitcoin through a Bitcoin ETF like ARKB—$25 a week.
- The Golden Rule: **Never sell—just keep buying.** Stay consistent, and let time and compounding grow your wealth over the long term.

When you need a down payment for real estate, you can borrow money tax-free for the down payment. For example, you might put 3% down and use house hacking (reread about it in Chapter 33)—buying a property to live in and another to rent.

This is a simple example, but the key is to decide what you want, write it down, and start working to make it happen.

I tell my students, "You're the luckiest people in the world." Why? Because just a few years ago, it was almost impossible for the average American to use a Buy, Borrow, Die strategy. But thanks to recent innovations, it's now possible.

Think about it:

- With an iPhone or Android, you can download apps like M1 Finance or Robinhood and buy fractional shares, even with just $25 or $50 a month, buying stocks and ETFs with no fees.
- Complex ETFs, like covered call ETFs, let a money manager trade options for you, so you don't have to learn how to do it yourself.
- The internet and YouTube make it easy to learn about different ETFs and their pros and cons.

For real estate:

- You can use Airbnb and VRBO to research short-term rentals and learn how to pay no taxes. Apps like REPStracker can help you understand the benefits of long-term, mid-term, and short-term rentals.

By reading this book, you're already ahead of 99.9% of people in the United States, and you know the strategy to use.

In the future, you can be your own financial advisor by mastering these strategies and giving yourself the best advice.

So keep learning and raising your financial IQ.

And remember, if you live in the United States, you're already one of the luckiest people in the world!

S.M.A.R.T. TIP

Be grateful for what you have.

Become financially free and help others do the same.

49

Will You Own Nothing and Be Happy?

own·er·ship

/ˈōnərˌSHip/

noun

the act, state, or right of possessing something

I came across some surprising statistics recently: Only 14% of adults have saved $100,000 for retirement, and 78% of Americans have less than $50,000 saved. Even if they save aggressively, after factoring in inflation and taxes, their retirement accounts will never deliver financial freedom. The 4% rule is my proof.

As we talked about back in Chapter 12, the 4% rule is a guideline for retirees to figure out how much they can safely withdraw from their retirement savings each year without running out of money. The idea is that if you withdraw 4% of your portfolio in the first year of retirement and then adjust for inflation, your savings should last about 30 years. Hopefully, you won't run out of money or live too long!

Let's say you've got $1 million in your retirement account right now. Sounds like a lot, right? But after taxes and inflation, are you really a millionaire?

According to the 4% rule, you could withdraw $40,000 in the first year. The next year, if inflation is 3%, you'd withdraw $41,200, and so on. If you're thinking, "That's not much money," you're right. And here's the kicker: The rule has been updated to just 3.3%. So now your $40,000 a year is down to $33,000, and there's still a 10% chance you'll run out of money!

It gets worse. When Americans realize they're short on retirement savings, they often meet with a financial advisor who tells them, "You need to save more in your retirement account and follow the 4% rule." But really? Is that the best they've got? Sadly, yes, it is. I used to be one of those advisors.

If I were in the meeting, I'd be asking the advisor some tough questions about their own retirement plans:

- "When do you feel you can retire, and how much do you have saved?"
- "What other income streams will you have, and how many are tax-free?"
- "Can you retire on just your retirement account, or are you relying on fees from mine to fund your retirement?"
- "What happens if AI or robots take over most jobs in the next 5 to 15 years? How will a retirement account help then?"
- "Since 401(k)s are tax-deferred, how does it help to defer taxes if withdrawals can trigger taxes on social security benefits?"

- "Do you own rental properties? Would you recommend house hacking as a strategy?"
- "Can you show me how to retire early and pay no taxes?"

I'm not saying you should actually confront them like this. Advisors are just like us—they're doing the best with the tools they have, trying to build a future for themselves and retire comfortably.

Still, when I heard the statement, "You will own nothing and be happy," it struck a chord. It made me realize how many Americans are in that exact situation-not truly owning much, just getting by. For many, even the dream of homeownership feels increasingly out of reach. It almost feels like the entire system is set up to keep them from owning anything.

This statement came from a video shown at a meeting at the World Economic Forum (WEF) in 2016. It was taken from an article, "Welcome to 2030; I Own Nothing, Have No Privacy, and Life Has Never Been Better," written by a Danish MP, Aida Auken.

Well, I've been there—owning nothing—and it's a horrible and scary feeling. After the 2008 financial crisis, it took me over a decade to dig myself out of the hole and resulted in a divorce and the loss of my home. Those were miserable times, and the stress was unbearable.

Part of the reason I wrote this book is to make sure you own stuff. You'll be happier when you do. Studies have shown that owning assets—whether financial, physical, or even social—can make you feel more secure and satisfied with life.

Here's what research says:

- **Financial security and happiness.** Owning assets like real estate, stocks, or a business is linked to greater happiness because it reduces financial stress and increases life satisfaction.
- **Homeownership.** Homeowners are generally happier than renters because owning a home gives you stability, a sense of belonging, and financial security through home equity.
- **Wealth and well-being.** Owning a diverse portfolio of assets usually leads to greater wealth and happiness, especially if you use that wealth to improve your life, not just accumulate it.
- **Psychological ownership.** The feeling that something is "yours," even if it's not a physical object, can contribute to your well-being.
- **Social and psychological benefits.** Owning assets can boost your social status and give you a sense of achievement and autonomy, adding to your happiness.

But remember, while owning assets can make you happier, it's not a guarantee. How you manage those assets and the context of your life—relationships, health, purpose—also play big roles in your overall happiness.

If you want to own stuff, the clock is ticking. You need to raise your financial IQ fast. If you're starting from scratch, you've got to learn quickly and start taking those first steps to understand the benefits and learn to judge the risk vs reward.

I also believe that owning Bitcoin, or a Bitcoin ETF, should be part of your plan. Bitcoin is decentralized and not controlled by the centralized banking system that has created "the haves and the have-nots."

Set a goal to buy real estate as soon as possible. If moving to a less expensive state with lower taxes is an option, do it. (I recently did exactly that, moving from California to Tennessee, and now I'm kicking myself that I didn't do it sooner.) If you don't buy in the next few years, it may become even harder. If you can only afford a $300,000 property (for example) with a 3% down payment, jump on it and perhaps you can rent a part of the property. Set a goal to rent it out and buy another with just 3% down. Do it a third time, and you'll start owning stuff that pays you income. And if Bitcoin hits $1 million by 2030 and $1 billion by 2038, you could own a lot more.

"So how will my retirement account help me?"

Great question. I don't think it will. You may be better off skipping the retirement account and creating your own "match" by learning to use the Borrow button, safely. As I noted in an earlier chapter, when I met Stella, she had a 401(k). Once she started using M1 Finance and the Borrow button, she decided to liquidate it and pay the penalties, and we focused on building income streams. It was one of the best financial decisions we ever made. We've built more passive income from investing in the past three years than I did in fifteen years as a financial advisor. Sadhguru was right: "Thinking is just recycling of the data you've gathered in the past." I had to change my thinking.

People often say I "think outside the box," and now I invite you to do the same. I've been inside the box, and I didn't like what I saw.

I believe anyone can learn the strategies we teach, and I've found they're the most effective way to build wealth and secure your financial future.

It took me over 25 years to learn all this. The great news is that I've boiled it down for you in this book, so it won't take you a quarter of a century! And if I find something better, I'll let you know. But so far, this is the best and most powerful strategy for building wealth and reducing your tax bill to ZERO.

Own stuff; you will be happier.
When you own stuff, give 10% to church and/or charity.

Epilogue

As we reach the end of this book, I hope I achieved my three goals:

- **Did you find it simple and easy to understand?** Making complex ideas simple isn't easy, but I poured my effort into writing this book in a way that anyone can follow. If you found it to be a simple and easy read, I'd love to hear about your success after putting these strategies to work.

- **Was it worth the cost of the book?** I aimed to deliver value in every chapter, whether through strategies that can help you save you huge amounts on taxes, make smarter investments, or both. If this book has given you even one actionable idea, I hope you'll agree it was a worthwhile investment—and if you take the time to master the strategies, I truly believe it could help you make and save millions.

- **Did it change your thinking?** If you find yourself nodding
  yes, then I consider it a success. My goal has been to
  offer you fresh ideas and perspectives to break free
  from old habits and beliefs, and to show that financial
  freedom is achievable—at any age. Now, it's up to you to
  take action and transform your financial future.

> If you'd like more guidance, please visit us at:
> **www.ThePerfectPortfolio.com**
> or check out our YouTube channel:
> **youtube.com/@P2Wealth**

We're constantly creating new content to simplify and
explain these strategies. Our mission is to help 1 million people
become millionaires—and we're dedicated to making it happen.
The question is: **Will you be one of them?**

Lastly, if you enjoyed this book, we'd truly appreciate it if
you shared it with others and left a five-star review on Amazon
or Goodreads. Thank you so much for buying and reading my
fourth book, coauthored with A.J. Merrifield.

Cheers!

—Mark and the team at The Perfect Portfolio

Real Estate Simplified

You can **buy** it with OPM, which is **tax-free**.

It appreciates **tax-free**.

You can depreciate it—to **reduce your taxes**.

You can "accelerate" the depreciation for **more tax-free income**.

Your rental income can be **tax-free**.

You can **borrow** from it, also **tax-free,** to **buy** other assets.

You can **borrow** from real estate to **buy** more real estate.

When you **die**, it can be passed **tax-free** to your heirs.

How to Get
Wealthy . . . Simplified

1. **Buy** Asset A.
2. As Asset A appreciates, **borrow** from it to **buy** Asset B.
3. As Asset B appreciates, **borrow** from it to **buy** Asset C.
4. As Asset C appreciates, **borrow** from it to **buy** Asset D.
5. As Asset D appreciates, **borrow** from it to **buy** Asset E.
6. As Asset E appreciates, **borrow** from it to **buy** Asset F.
7. As Asset F appreciates, **borrow** from it to **buy** Asset A.

8. As Asset A continues to appreciate, borrow from Asset A to buy more of Asset B.
9. As Asset B continues to appreciate, borrow from Asset B to buy more of Asset C.
10. As Asset C continues to appreciate, borrow from Asset C to buy more of Asset D.
11. As Asset D continues to appreciate, borrow from Asset D to buy more of Asset E.

12. As Asset E continues to appreciate, borrow from Asset E to buy more of Asset F.

13. As Asset F continues to appreciate, borrow from Asset F to buy more of Asset A.

14. If Asset A crashes but Asset B didn't, borrow from Asset B to buy more of Asset A.

15. If Asset B crashes but Asset C didn't, borrow from Asset C to buy more of Asset B.

16. If Asset C crashes but Asset D didn't, borrow from Asset D to buy more of Asset C.

17. If Asset D crashes but Asset E didn't, borrow from Asset E to buy more of Asset D.

18. If Asset E crashes but Asset F didn't, borrow from Asset F to buy more of Asset E.

19. If Asset F crashes but Asset A didn't, borrow from Asset A to buy more of Asset F.

20. Go back to Step 1. Lather, rinse, and repeat.

Glossary of Terms

401(k). A retirement savings plan offered by employers that allows employees to save and invest pre-tax income.

Example: "Contributing to his 401(k) helped him grow his retirement savings tax-deferred."

529 Plan. A tax-advantaged savings plan designed to encourage saving for future education costs.

Example: "She opened a 529 plan to save for her children's college expenses."

Appreciation. The increase in the value of an asset over time.

Example: "The appreciation of the property added to their net worth significantly."

Asset. Anything valuable that can generate income or increase in value, like stocks or real estate.

Example: "Investing in an income-generating asset, like rental property, is a smart financial move."

Asset Protection. Strategies used to guard wealth from lawsuits, creditors, and taxes.

Example: "He set up a trust as a form of asset protection for his estate."

Backdoor Roth IRA. A method for high-income earners to contribute to a Roth IRA indirectly.

Example: "He used the backdoor Roth IRA strategy to get around contribution limits."

Bear Market. A market in which prices are falling, encouraging selling.

Example: "During a bear market, many investors tend to panic and sell."

Bitcoin. A type of cryptocurrency that operates without a central authority.

Example: "He invested in Bitcoin as a hedge against inflation."

Bond. A debt investment where an investor loans money to a government or corporation in exchange for periodic interest payments.

Example: "Bonds provide a stable income stream for conservative investors."

Borrowing Against Assets. Using assets as collateral to secure a loan without selling them.

Example: "Instead of selling his stocks, he was borrowing against those assets to buy more real estate."

Brokerage Account. An account that allows individuals to buy and sell securities.

Example: "He opened a brokerage account to start investing in stocks and ETFs."

Bull Market. A market in which prices are rising, encouraging buying.

Example: "During a bull market, investors feel optimistic and tend to buy more."

Buy, Borrow, Die Strategy. A wealth-building method that involves buying assets, borrowing against them, and passing them to heirs tax-free.

Example: "The Buy, Borrow, Die strategy allows families to accumulate wealth while avoiding capital gains taxes."

Call Option. A financial contract that gives the holder the right to buy an asset at a set price.

Example: "He purchased a call option to potentially profit from a rise in stock price."

Capital Gains. The profit from selling an asset, like stocks or property, that has increased in value.

Example: "You'll owe capital gains taxes if you sell that stock for a profit."

Capital Gains Tax. A tax on the profit made from selling an asset that has increased in value.

Example: "He sold his stocks for a profit and was hit with a capital gains tax."

Cash Flow. The total amount of money being transferred into and out of a business or investment.

Example: "The rental property generates a positive cash flow each month."

Certificate of Deposit (CD). A savings certificate with a fixed maturity date and interest rate.

Example: "She locked in a higher interest rate with a five-year CD."

Compounding. The process whereby interest is credited to an existing principal amount as well as to interest already paid.

Example: "Compounding allows your savings to grow faster over"

Cost Segregation. A tax strategy used to accelerate depreciation of certain assets to reduce taxes.

Example: "Cost segregation helped them write off more of their property costs in the early years."

Covered Call. A strategy where an investor sells a call option on a stock they own.

Example: "He sold covered calls to generate extra income from his stockholdings."

Credit Risk. The risk that a borrower will default on a loan.

Example: "Investors demand higher interest rates to compensate for credit risk."

Cryptocurrency. A digital currency that uses cryptography for security.

Example: "Many investors are adding cryptocurrency like Bitcoin to their portfolios."

Dead Money. Money that is invested but cannot be used to take a loan secured by that investment.

Example: "Any money that cannot be borrowed against is considered dead money, as it cannot be leveraged to acquire other assets."

Deduction. An expense that can be subtracted from taxable income, reducing the total taxes owed.

Example: "Contributing to a retirement account can lead to a substantial tax deduction."

Depreciation. The reduction in the value of an asset over time, often used for tax deductions.

Example: "He claimed depreciation on his rental property to lower his taxable income."

Diversification. Spreading investments across different assets to reduce risk.

Example: "A diversified portfolio helps manage risk by balancing different kinds of investments."

Dividend. A distribution of profits by a corporation to its shareholders.

Example: "Holding dividend-paying stocks can provide regular income in addition to growth."

Dividend Yield. A financial ratio that shows how much a company pays out in dividends each year relative to its stock price.

Example: "A high dividend yield can be attractive to income-seeking investors."

Dollar-Cost Averaging. Investing a fixed amount regularly to reduce the impact of volatility.

Example: "By using dollar-cost averaging, she minimized the risks of market timing."

Dow Jones Industrial Average (DJIA). A stock market index that measures the performance of 30 large companies listed on US stock exchanges.

Example: "The DJIA is often used as a barometer for the overall health of the US stock market."

Equity. Ownership of assets that may have debts or other liabilities attached to them.

Example: "He built equity in his home by paying off the mortgage."

ETF (Exchange-Traded Fund). A type of investment fund traded on stock exchanges that holds assets like stocks or bonds.

Example: "Investing in an ETF can give you exposure to multiple stocks in a single trade."

Fiduciary Advisor. A financial advisor legally required to act in their clients' best interests.

Example: "A fiduciary advisor is bound to prioritize their clients' needs over their own commission."

Fiscal Policy. Government policies regarding taxation and spending that impact the economy.

Example: "Expansionary fiscal policy can stimulate economic growth during a recession."

Fractional Reserve Banking. A banking system where banks hold only a fraction of their deposits as reserves, and multiply the money supply by creating many times the amount deposited through a process called the deposit multiplier.

Example: "Fractional reserve banking allows banks to lend up to ten times more than they actually hold in cash, just by creating bank entries in their ledgers."

Gold Standard. A system where currency is tied directly to gold.

Example: "Under the gold standard, every dollar was backed by a set amount of gold."

Good Debt Vs Bad Debt. Good debt is used to acquire assets that increase in value, while bad debt involves liabilities with no return.

Example: "Using a mortgage to buy a rental property is considered good debt."

Hedge. An investment made to reduce the risk of adverse price movements in an asset.

Example: "Gold is often used as a hedge against inflation."

Index Fund. A type of mutual fund or ETF designed to track the performance of a specific market index.

Example: "Index funds are a low-cost way to invest in the stock market."

Inflation. The rate at which the general price level for goods and services rises.

Example: "Inflation erodes purchasing power, making things more expensive over time."

Initial Public Offering (IPO). The first time a company offers its stock to the public.

Example: "The company's IPO generated a lot of interest from investors."

Interest Rate. The percentage charged on a loan or paid on savings.

Example: "Rising interest rates can make borrowing more expensive."

Intrinsic Value. The actual worth of an asset, based on fundamental analysis.

Example: "He believes the intrinsic value of the stock is higher than its current market price."

IRA (Individual Retirement Account). A tax-advantaged account for retirement savings.

Example: "She contributes to both a traditional and a Roth IRA to maximize her tax savings."

IUL (Indexed Universal Life Insurance). A type of life insurance that puts a risk-free market-linked CD inside a life-insurance policy, allowing risk-free and tax-free investing.

Example: "With an IUL, you can borrow against the cash value without paying taxes."

Leverage. Using borrowed money to increase the potential return on an investment.

Example: "Leverage allows investors to buy more assets than they could with their own funds."

Liquidity. The ability of an asset to be quickly converted into cash without significant loss in value.

Example: "Stocks are considered liquid assets because they can be sold quickly."

Margin Loan. A loan secured by an investment portfolio that allows investors to access funds without liquidating the assets in the portfolio and triggering taxes.

Example: "Instead of selling his shares, he took out a margin loan to buy more stock."

Municipal Bond. A bond issued by a local government that often provides tax-free interest income.

Example: "A municipal bond is a popular choice for investors seeking tax-free income."

Mutual Fund. An investment vehicle made up of a pool of funds collected from many investors to invest in securities.

Example: "Mutual funds allow investors to diversify even with small initial investments."

Net Worth. The value of a person's assets minus their liabilities.

Example: "By paying down debt and growing investments, he increased his net worth."

Noncorrelated Assets. Investments that don't move in sync with one another, providing diversification.

Example: "Gold and stocks are noncorrelated assets, offering balance in a portfolio."

OPM (Other People's Money). The concept of using borrowed funds or capital to make investments.

Example: "Using OPM, they purchased more properties without using their own savings."

Options. Financial contracts that give the buyer the right, but not the obligation, to buy or sell an asset at a specified price.

Example: "Options can be used to hedge risk or speculate on price movements."

Passive Income. Earnings that require little or no effort to maintain, like rental income or dividends.

Example: "Investing in rental properties provides a steady stream of passive income."

Pension. A retirement plan that provides a monthly income in retirement.

Example: "He relied on his pension and social security to cover his living expenses in retirement."

Pillar. One of the core asset classes or strategies in the Buy Borrow Die strategy that forms the foundation of wealth-building.

Example: "The Five Pillars of the Buy Borrow Die strategy include stocks, real estate, life insurance, cryptocurrency, and precious metals."

Portfolio. A range of investments held by an individual or institution.

Example: "A well-diversified portfolio helps manage investment risk."

Precious Metals. Valuable metals like gold and silver, often used as a hedge against inflation.

Example: "Precious metals like gold offer a stable store of value during economic downturns."

Quantitative Easing. When the government prints money (and causes inflation).

Example: "The Federal Reserve used quantitative easing to help stimulate the economy after the financial crisis."

Real Estate Professional Status (REPS). A tax designation allowing individuals in real estate to claim significant deductions.

Example: "By qualifying for REPS, they were able to offset much of their income with real estate losses."

Rider. An add-on or adjustment to an insurance policy that provides additional benefits beyond the basic coverage.

Example: "He added a chronic illness rider to his life insurance policy, allowing him to access funds if he becomes seriously ill."

Risk Tolerance. An investor's ability or willingness to endure potential losses.

Example: "Her high risk tolerance allows her to invest in more volatile assets."

Roth Conversion. The process of converting a traditional IRA into a Roth IRA, paying taxes on the converted amount now for tax-free withdrawals later.

Example: "He decided to do a Roth conversion while his income was lower to reduce future tax bills."

Roth IRA. A retirement account funded with after-tax dollars, offering tax-free growth and withdrawals.

Example: "A Roth IRA allows you to take out your retirement savings tax-free."

S&P 500. A stock market index that tracks the stock performance of 500 large companies listed on stock exchanges in the US.

Example: "Investors often use the S&P 500 as a benchmark for the overall market performance."

Step-Up in Basis. A tax rule that allows heirs to inherit assets at their current market value, minimizing capital gains taxes.

Example: "The step-up in basis allows heirs to avoid paying taxes on the appreciation during the original owner's lifetime."

Stock. A share of ownership in a company.

Example: "Buying stocks in companies with high growth potential is a key strategy for building wealth."

Tax-Loss Harvesting. Selling investments at a loss to offset capital gains and reduce taxes.

Example: "He used tax-loss harvesting to reduce his taxable income by selling underperforming stocks."

Term Insurance. Life insurance that provides coverage for a specific term or period.

Example: "Term insurance is a cost-effective way to ensure your family's financial security."

Yield. The income returned on an investment, typically expressed as a percentage.

Example: "The stock's high yield made it an attractive investment for income-focused investors."

Bonus Stock Report

Here are the top 10 stocks that performed best over the past 30-years. (This list is as of the writing of this book in September 2024. Remember, past performance doesn't guarantee future performance or returns.)

1. **NVIDIA (NVDA).** NVIDIA has been the top-performing stock, with $10,000 investment 25 years ago now worth over $32 million. The company's success is driven by its innovations in graphics processing units (GPUs) and AI technology. (30 year return: 322,185%*)

2. **Amazon (AMZN).** From an online bookstore to a global e-commerce and cloud computing giant, Amazon has achieved phenomenal growth. (30 year return: 249,208%*)

3. **Monster Beverage (MNST).** Known for its energy drinks, Monster Beverage has turned a $10,000 investment into approximately $16 million. (30 year return: 164,539%*)

4. **NVR Inc. (NVR).** NVR, Inc. engages in the construction and sale of single-family detached homes, townhomes, and condominium buildings. (30 year return: 140,431%*)

5. **Apple (AAPL).** Apple's consistent innovation and product success have made it one of the most valuable companies globally. Similar to Monster Beverage's trajectory, a $10,000 investment in Apple would be worth millions today. (30 year return: 88,807%*)

6. **Netflix (NFLX).** Revolutionizing entertainment consumption with streaming services, Netflix has seen substantial growth. (30 year return: 58,273%*)

7. **Pool Corp. (POOL).** Pool Corp. engages in the wholesale distribution of swimming pool supplies, equipment, and related leisure products. (30 year return: 56,328%*)

8. **Axon Enterprise Inc. (AXON).** Axon Enterprise, Inc. engages in the development, manufacture, and sale of conducted electrical weapons for personal defense, including the TASER line of defense products. (30 year return: 56,082%*)

9. **Biogen Inc. (BIIB).** Biogen, Inc. is a biopharmaceutical company, which engages in discovering, developing, and delivering therapies for neurological and neurodegenerative diseases. (30 year return: 50,397%*)

10. **Altria Group Inc. (MO).** Altria Group, Inc. is a holding company which engages in the manufacture and sale of cigarettes in the United States. (30 year return: 49,365%*)

These companies have not only delivered significant returns but also shaped their respective industries through innovation and strategic growth.

(*Data is from August 1994 through July 2024. Source: *U.S. News*, August 27, 2024.)

Here are the top 10 stocks that performed best over the past 10-years. In the past decade, some of the same names as in the list above continue to shine, while others have emerged as new leaders.

1. **NVIDIA Corporation (NVDA).** Gains further prominence with AI and data center applications. (10 year return: 27,432%**)

2. **Celsius Holdings Inc. (CELH).** American company that produces a range of fitness and energy beverages under the brand name *Celsius*. (10 year return: 18,678%**)

3. **Advanced Micro Devices (AMD).** AMD is a leading semiconductor company known for its high-performance CPUs, GPUs, and AI-driven hardware solutions, driving innovation across gaming, data centers, and computing. (10 year return: 4,712%**)

4. **Builders FirstSource Inc. (BLDR).** The largest supplier of building products, prefabricated components and value-added services in the US. (10 year return: 3,457%**)

5. **Fair Isaac Corp (FICO).** American data analytics company based in Bozeman, Montana, focused on credit scoring services. (10 year return: 3,434%**)

6. **Comfort Systems USA Inc. (FIX).** A leading building and service provider for mechanical, electrical and plumbing building systems. (10 year return: 3,008%**)

7. **Axon Enterprise Inc. (AXON).** American company based in Scottsdale, Arizona that develops technology and weapons products for military, law enforcement, and civilians. (10 year return: 2,487%**)

8. **Broadcom Inc. (AVGO).** American multinational designer, developer, manufacturer, and global supplier of a wide range of semiconductor and infrastructure software products. (10 year return: 2,468%**)

9. **Monolithic Power Systems Inc. (MPWR).** Provides power circuits for systems found in cloud computing, telecom infrastructures, automotive, industrial applications and consumer applications. (10 year return: 2,203%**)

10. **Coca-Cola Consolidated Inc. (COKE).** The company makes, sells and distributes Coca-Cola products along with other beverages, distributing to a market of 65 million people in 14 states. (10 year return: 1,793%**)

(**Data is from September 2014 through September 2024. Source: YCharts, October 4, 2024.)

Here are the top 10 dividend stocks from the S&P 500 (those paying the highest dividends):

1. **Walgreens Boots Alliance (WBA).** 12.14% dividend yield***. Despite recent challenges, it remains a high-yield stock.

2. **Altria Group (MO).** 7.07% dividend yield***, known for its consistent dividends in the tobacco sector.
3. **Pfizer (PFE).** 6.74% dividend yield***, known for it's pharmaceutical products.
4. **LyondellBassell Industries (LYB).** 6.50% dividend yield***, a global chemical company.
5. **Verizon Communications (VZ).** 6.6% dividend yield***, a reliable telecom dividend stock.
6. **Dow (DOW).** 6.37% dividend yield***, benefiting from its steady telecom operations.
7. **Franklin Resources (BEN).** 5.73% dividend yield***, a global investment firm.
8. **Healthpeak Properties (DOC).** 5.6% dividend yield***, a Real Estate Investment Trust (REIT) that specializes in healthcare properties.
9. **Ford Motor (F).** 5.59% dividend yield***, one of the "Big Three" US automakers.
10. **Realty Income (O).** 5.56% dividend yield***, REIT that specializes in single-tenant commercial properties.

These dividends are considered "high" but not when compared with the dividends offered from complex ETFs.

(***Data is from November 21, 2024. Source: Kiplinger Personal Finance, November 21, 2024.)

Knowledge Quiz and Study Guide

Multiple-Choice Questions

1. Who is the book primarily dedicated to?
   A. Experienced investors
   B. Financial advisors
   C. The average American worker
   D. Politicians

2. What is the central theme of the book?
   A. How to get rich quickly through day trading
   B. How to achieve financial independence and minimize taxes legally
   C. The history of the US tax code
   D. The dangers of using credit cards

3. According to the author, what was his motivation for writing the book?
   A. To become a famous author
   B. To share simple but effective strategies to achieve financial independence at any age
   C. To promote his financial advising business
   D. To criticize traditional financial advice

4. What is the author's opinion of traditional retirement accounts like 401(k)s?
   A. They are the least effective way to build wealth and avoid taxes. (They suck.)
   B. Everyone should maximize their contributions to these accounts.
   C. They are too risky for most investors.
   D. They should be eliminated.

5. What does the acronym "OPM" stand for in the context of the book?
   A. Other people's money
   B. Optimal portfolio management
   C. Outstanding payment mortgage
   D. Overt profit maximization

6. What is the core concept of the Buy, Borrow, Die strategy?
   A. Inheriting wealth from wealthy relatives
   B. Avoiding all forms of debt
   C. Acquiring assets and leveraging them to buy more assets while minimizing taxes
   D. Investing only in high-risk, high-reward assets

7. What are The Five Pillars of the Buy, Borrow, Die strategy?
    A. Stocks, bonds, mutual funds, real estate, gold
    B. Stocks and ETFs, real estate, life insurance, cryptocurrency, gold and precious metals
    C. Savings accounts, 401(k)s, IRAs, annuities, bonds
    D. Education, mentorship, networking, hard work, discipline

8. What is "dead money" according to the author?
    A. Money lost in a bad investment
    B. Money kept in a low-interest savings account
    C. Money invested in assets you cannot borrow against
    D. Money spent on unnecessary expenses

9. What is the author's view on debt?
    A. All debt is bad and should be avoided.
    B. Debt used strategically to acquire appreciating assets can build wealth.
    C. Only the wealthy can benefit from using debt.
    D. Debt is only acceptable for purchasing a primary residence.

10. How does the author define "financial alchemy"?
    A. Turning everyday items into valuable assets
    B. Using illegal means to avoid paying taxes
    C. Transforming "bad debt" into "good debt" by using it for investments
    D. Predicting market movements with 100% accuracy

11. Why does the author suggest that traditional financial advice often benefits financial institutions more than the individual?

   A. Financial advisors are inherently dishonest.

   B. Financial advisors often promote products that generate the most commissions or that benefit their employers.

   C. Individuals are not capable of managing their own finances.

   D. The financial system is rigged against individual investors.

12. What is the main advantage of an S-Corp for small business owners, according to the book?

   A. It allows for dividing income into salary and distributions, potentially reducing self-employment taxes.

   B. It eliminates the need to pay any taxes.

   C. It simplifies the process of applying for business loans.

   D. It provides better legal protection for business owners.

13. How does the author suggest making education a business expense?

A. Only taking courses directly related to your current job

B. Investing in education that enhances your skills and knowledge to grow your business, making the costs deductible

C. Deducting the cost of any books or online courses on your tax return

D. Attending conferences and seminars in exotic locations

14. What is the author's recommendation for handling health insurance premiums as a small business owner?

A. Avoid getting health insurance.

B. Choose the cheapest plan available, even if it has limited coverage.

C. Deduct 100% of the premiums as a business expense to reduce taxable income.

D. Negotiate a lower premium with your insurance provider.

15. What is the key takeaway from the author's discussion of fiat currency?
   A. Fiat currency is backed by gold and therefore a stable investment.
   B. Fiat currency is only valuable because the government maintains it and because the people have faith in its value.
   C. Fiat currency is the most efficient form of money.
   D. Fiat currency is accepted globally and therefore the best currency to use.

16. What example does the author use to illustrate the concept of fractional reserve banking?
   A. A baker trading bread for services
   B. An individual depositing money into a bank, which keeps a small fraction of deposits in reserve and loans out the rest, creating money and expanding the money supply.
   C. A government printing more money to stimulate the economy
   D. An individual investing in the stock market

17. Which characteristic does the author believe is MOST important for something to be considered money?
   A. Backed by a physical commodity
   B. Issued by a government
   C. In limited supply
   D. Universally recognized

18. What is one of the potential risks of fractional reserve banking, as discussed in the book?
   A. It can lead to deflation, making goods and services cheaper.
   B. It can lead to inflation if the money supply expands too quickly.
   C. It discourages people from taking out loans.
   D. It makes it difficult for banks to make a profit.

19. What is the author's opinion on "diversification" as typically recommended by financial advisors?
   A. Diversification is the most important factor in investing.
   B. Only diversify across different types of index funds.
   C. True diversification is not a traditional portfolio of stocks and bonds.
   D. Diversification is unnecessary for experienced investors.

20. What example does the author give to illustrate the potential benefits of leveraged ETFs?
   A. Investing in a bond ETF during a period of rising interest rates
   B. Investing in a gold ETF during a period of high inflation
   C. Investing in SPXL, a 3x leveraged S&P 500 ETF, during the market downturn of March 2020
   D. Investing in an inverse ETF during a bull market

21. What are covered call ETFs?
    A. ETFs that invest in companies that have a history of issuing covered calls
    B. ETFs that utilize a covered call options strategy to generate income
    C. ETFs that exclusively invest in call options
    D. ETFs designed to protect against losses during a market downturn

22. What is a potential advantage of using covered call ETFs, as mentioned in the book?
    A. They eliminate market risk.
    B. They provide guaranteed returns.
    C. They can generate monthly income for investors through option premiums.
    D. They are tax-free investments.

23. What is a potential drawback of synthetic covered call ETFs?
    A. They are not available to individual investors.
    B. They are highly illiquid investments.
    C. They can be complex and less transparent due to the use of derivatives.
    D. They are only available through a select few brokerage firms.

24. Why does the author encourage readers to become "sophisticated investors"?
A. To impress financial advisors with their knowledge
B. To engage in high-frequency trading and exploit market inefficiencies
C. To identify and take advantage of investment opportunities that traditional advisors might not present
D. To become financially independent without relying on any external advice

25. What is the primary benefit of a Roth IRA, as highlighted in the book?
A. Contributions are tax-deductible in the year they are made.
B. Withdrawals in retirement are tax-free.
C. There are no income limitations to contribute.
D. It allows for unlimited contributions.

26. What is the backdoor Roth IRA strategy?
A. A way to withdraw money from a Roth IRA penalty-free before age 59½
B. A way to contribute to a Roth IRA even if your income exceeds the limit
C. A way to invest in assets not typically allowed in a Roth IRA, like real estate
D. A way to avoid paying taxes on Roth IRA contributions

27. Why does the author compare understanding taxes with learning a new language?

    A. The tax code is intentionally designed to be confusing.

    B. Mastering the language of taxes can help you legally minimize your tax burden.

    C. Only tax professionals can understand the complexities of the tax code.

    D. Speaking about taxes is as enjoyable as learning a new language.

28. What is the difference between short-term and long-term capital gains taxes?

    A. Short-term capital gains are taxed at a lower rate than long-term capital gains.

    B. Short-term capital gains are taxed as ordinary income, while long-term capital gains are taxed at a lower rate.

    C. Short-term capital gains apply to assets held for less than one year, while long-term capital gains apply to assets held for more than five years.

    D. There is no difference; both are taxed at the same rate.

29. What is the main tax advantage of owning a primary residence, as discussed in the book?
  A. Property taxes are deductible on your federal income tax return.
  B. Rental income from a portion of your primary residence is tax-free.
  C. Profits from the sale of a primary residence are always tax-free.
  D. You can deduct the interest paid on your mortgage.

30. What is cost segregation in real estate investing?
  A. A method of lowering property taxes by challenging the assessed value
  B. A strategy for accelerating depreciation deductions on a rental property
  C. A way to divide the costs of a property among multiple investors
  D. A technique for negotiating a lower purchase price on a property

31. Why is cost segregation a beneficial tax strategy for real estate investors?
  A. It eliminates capital gains taxes on the sale of a property.
  B. It allows investors to deduct the entire cost of the property in the year it is purchased.
  C. It increases tax-free cash flow in the early years of ownership.
  D. It defers taxes on rental income indefinitely.

32. What is the main advantage of the Augusta Rule, as described in the book?

    A. It allows homeowners in Augusta, Georgia, to avoid paying property taxes.

    B. It allows homeowners to rent out their primary residence for up to 14 days per year and receive the rental income tax-free.

    C. It provides tax deductions for expenses related to hosting guests in your home.

    D. It exempts homeowners from capital gains taxes on the sale of a vacation property.

33. What is a life insurance rider?

    A. A type of life insurance that covers motorcycle accidents

    B. An optional add-on to a life insurance policy that provides additional benefits

    C. A requirement for purchasing a life insurance policy

    D. A type of life insurance only available to high net worth individuals

34. What does the acronym "TCCC" stand for in the context of life insurance riders?

    A. Total comprehensive coverage clause

    B. Terminal illness rider, chronic illness rider, critical illness rider, conversion rider

    C. Term conversion, cash collection, coverage continuation

    D. Trust creation, charitable contribution, conversion option

35. What is indexed universal life insurance (IUL)?
  A. A type of term life insurance
  B. A type of permanent life insurance with a cash value component linked to a stock market index
  C. A high-risk investment disguised as life insurance
  D. A type of life insurance only available through employers

36. How does the author describe IUL in terms of its investment features?
  A. As the "Swiss army knife of investing" due to its flexibility and features
  B. As too complex and risky for most investors
  C. As inferior to traditional investment options like mutual funds
  D. As a guaranteed way to beat the market

37. What is the author's perspective on the Buy Term and Invest the Difference strategy?
  A. It is always the best approach to life insurance.
  B. While it can work for some, it might not be the most tax-efficient way to build wealth.
  C. It is too risky for most investors.
  D. It should only be used by experienced investors.

38. What is a potential advantage of using an IUL as a tax-free family bank?

   A. It allows policyholders to withdraw money from the policy tax-free at any time.

   B. It allows for tax-free loans against the policy's cash value, which can be used for various purposes.

   C. It provides a guaranteed return on investment.

   D. It eliminates the need to pay taxes on other sources of income.

39. According to the author, which of the following characteristics does Bitcoin share with the traditional definition of money?

   A. It is backed by a physical commodity.

   B. It is issued and controlled by a central bank.

   C. It is easily transferable.

   D. It is a stable store of value.

40. Why does the author believe that owning assets can contribute to happiness?

   A. Material possessions are the ultimate source of joy.

   B. Owning assets allows you to buy anything you want.

   C. Owning assets provides financial security and a sense of belonging and reduces financial stress, which can improve overall well-being.

   D. Owning assets elevates your social status and impresses others.

41. According to the author, how can understanding correlation in investments be beneficial?

A. It helps predict market movements accurately.

B. It allows you to eliminate investment risk.

C. It helps create a more resilient portfolio that can withstand market fluctuations.

D. It ensures that all assets in your portfolio will increase in value simultaneously.

42. What is the key takeaway from the author's hypothetical example of inheriting $3 million in stock?

A. Inheritance is the easiest way to achieve financial independence.

B. Investing in a concentrated portfolio of just five stocks is a high-risk, high-reward strategy.

C. The "live off the Borrow button" concept demonstrates how to generate tax-free income from a portfolio without selling assets.

D. It is impossible to achieve financial independence without inheriting wealth.

43. What is the author's stance on "retirement," as traditionally defined?

A. Everyone should aim to retire by age 65.

B. Retirement should be the primary goal of financial planning.

C. Retirement is a Wall Street concept, designed to make people think they have to work until they're 65 or 70, pay taxes, and stash money in a retirement account.

D. Retirement is only achievable for the wealthy.

44. What advice does the author give to new investors?
  A. Invest all your money in a single, high-growth stock.
  B. Focus on short-term trading to make quick profits.
  C. Avoid investing until you have a substantial amount of money saved.
  D. Start small, diversify across different asset classes, and never stop learning.

45. What is the author's final message to readers?
  A. Becoming wealthy is easy and requires little effort.
  B. Traditional financial advice is always the best path to follow.
  C. Anyone can achieve financial independence by using the strategies outlined in the book and continually improving their financial IQ.
  D. It is impossible to avoid paying taxes legally.

46. What does S.M.A.R.T. stand for in the context of the book?
  A. Strategies to Maximize Assets and Reduce Taxes
  B. Simple Methods for Accumulating Retirement Treasures
  C. Smart Money Avoidance and Retirement Tactics
  D. Secure, Maximize, Accumulate, Reinvest, Transfer

47. What is the author's suggestion for handling a 401(k) after leaving a job?

A. Always roll it over to an IRA.

B. Explore options for managing taxes strategically, rather than defaulting to traditional advice.

C. Withdraw the funds immediately to avoid potential market losses.

D. Leave it with the former employer and hope for the best.

48. What is the author's view on the need for financial advisors?

A. Financial advisors are essential for everyone.

B. Individuals can become their own financial advisors by educating themselves and taking control of their finances.

C. Only the wealthy need financial advisors.

D. Financial advisors are only interested in making money for themselves.

49. Why does the author criticize the statement, "You will own nothing and be happy"?

A. He believes it promotes a socialist agenda.

B. He believes owning assets contributes to happiness and security, and that this statement suggests a future where individuals lack ownership and control.

C. He thinks it discourages people from working hard.

D. He believes it is unrealistic to think that people can be happy without owning anything.

E. All the above.

50. Why does the author believe that people should "own stuff"?

A. Owning stuff makes you superior to others.

B. You'll be happier.

C. It is the only way to impress friends and family.

D. It is the key to achieving lasting happiness.

Knowledge Quiz and Study Guide Answer Key

1. Who is the book primarily dedicated to?
   C. The average American worker

2. What is the central theme of the book?
   B. How to achieve financial independence and minimize taxes legally

3. According to the author, what was his motivation for writing the book?
   B. To share a simple but effective strategies to achieve financial independence at any age

4. What is the author's opinion of traditional retirement accounts like 401(k)s?
   A. They are the least effective way to build wealth and avoid taxes. (They suck.)

5. What does the acronym OPM stand for in the context of the book?
   A. Other people's money

6. What is the core concept of the Buy, Borrow, Die strategy?

   C. Acquiring assets and leveraging them to buy more assets while minimizing taxes

7. What are The Five Pillars of the Buy, Borrow, Die strategy?

   B. Stocks and ETFs, real estate, life insurance, cryptocurrency, gold and precious metals

8. What is "dead money" according to the author?

   C. Money invested in assets you cannot borrow against

9. What is the author's view on debt?

   B. Debt used strategically to acquire appreciating assets can build wealth.

10. How does the author define "financial alchemy"?

   C. Transforming "bad debt" into "good debt" by using it for investments

11. Why does the author suggest that traditional financial advice often benefits financial institutions more than the individual?

   B. Financial advisors often promote products that generate the most commissions or that benefit their employers.

12. What is the main advantage of an S-Corp for small business owners, according to the book?

   A. It allows for dividing income into salary and distributions, potentially reducing self-employment taxes.

13. How does the author suggest making education a business expense?

    B. Investing in education that enhances your skills and knowledge to grow your business, making the costs deductible.

14. What is the author's recommendation for handling health insurance premiums as a small business owner?

    C. Deduct 100% of the premiums as a business expense to reduce taxable income.

15. What is the key takeaway from the author's discussion of fiat currency?

    B. Fiat currency is only valuable because the government maintains it and because the people have faith in its value.

16. What example does the author use to illustrate the concept of fractional reserve banking?

    B. An individual depositing money into a bank, which keeps a small fraction of deposits in reserve and loans out the rest, creating money and expanding the money supply.

17. Which characteristic does the author believe is MOST important for something to be considered money?

    C. In limited supply

18. What is one of the potential risks of fractional reserve banking, as discussed in the book?

    B. It can lead to inflation if the money supply expands too quickly.

19. What is the author's opinion on "diversification" as
    typically recommended by financial advisors?
    C. True diversification is not a traditional portfolio of
    stocks and bonds.

20. What example does the author give to illustrate the
    potential benefits of leveraged ETFs?
    C. Investing in SPXL, a 3x leveraged S&P 500 ETF,
    during the market downturn of March 2020

21. What are covered call ETFs?
    B. ETFs that utilize a covered call options strategy to
    generate income

22. What is a potential advantage of using covered call
    ETFs, as mentioned in the book?
    C. They can generate monthly income for investors
    through option premiums.

23. What is a potential drawback of synthetic covered call
    ETFs?
    C. They can be complex and less transparent due to
    the use of derivatives.

24. Why does the author encourage readers to become
    "sophisticated investors"?
    C. To identify and take advantage of investment
    opportunities that traditional advisors might not
    present.

25. What is the primary benefit of a Roth IRA, as
    highlighted in the book?
    B. Withdrawals in retirement are tax-free.

26. What is the backdoor Roth IRA strategy?
  B. A way to contribute to a Roth IRA even if your income exceeds the limit.

27. Why does the author compare understanding taxes to learning a new language?
  B. Mastering the language of taxes can help you legally minimize your tax burden.

28. What is the difference between short-term and long-term capital gains taxes?
  B. Short-term capital gains are taxed as ordinary income, while long-term capital gains are taxed at a lower rate.

29. What is the main tax advantage of owning a primary residence, as discussed in the book?
  C. You can deduct the interest paid on your mortgage.

30. What is cost segregation in real estate investing?
  B. A strategy for accelerating depreciation deductions on a rental property

31. Why is cost segregation a beneficial tax strategy for real estate investors?
  C. It increases tax-free cash flow in the early years of ownership.

32. What is the main advantage of the "Augusta Rule," as described in the book?
  B. It allows homeowners to rent out their primary residence for up to 14 days per year and receive the rental income tax-free.

33. What is a life insurance rider?
    B. An optional add-on to a life insurance policy that provides additional benefits

34. What does the acronym "TCCC" stand for in the context of life insurance riders?
    B. Terminal illness rider, chronic illness rider, critical illness rider, conversion rider

35. What is indexed universal life insurance (IUL)?
    B. A type of permanent life insurance with a cash value component linked to a stock market index.

36. How does the author describe IUL in terms of its investment features?
    A. As the "Swiss army knife of investing" due to its flexibility and features

37. What is the author's perspective on the Buy Term and Invest the Difference strategy?
    B. While it can work for some, it might not be the most tax-efficient way to build wealth.

38. What is a potential advantage of using an IUL as a tax-free family bank?
    B. It allows for tax-free loans against the policy's cash value, which can be used for various purposes.

39. According to the author, which of the following characteristics does Bitcoin share with the traditional definition of money?
    C. It is easily transferable.

40. Why does the author believe that owning assets can contribute to happiness?

    C. Owning assets provides financial security and a sense of belonging and reduces financial stress, which can improve overall well-being.

41. According to the author, how can understanding correlation in investments be beneficial?

    C. It helps create a more resilient portfolio that can withstand market fluctuations.

42. What is the key takeaway from the author's hypothetical example of inheriting $3 million in stock?

    C. The "live off the Borrow button" concept demonstrates how to generate tax-free income from a portfolio without selling assets.

43. What is the author's stance on "retirement," as traditionally defined?

    C. Retirement is a Wall Street concept, designed to make people think they have to work until they're 65 or 70, pay taxes, and stash money in a retirement account.

44. What advice does the author give to new investors?

    D. Start small, diversify across different asset classes, and never stop learning.

45. What is the author's final message to readers?

    C. Anyone can achieve financial independence by using the strategies outlined in the book and continually improving their financial IQ.

46. What does S.M.A.R.T. stand for in the context of the book?

    A. Strategies to Maximize Assets and Reduce Taxes

47. What is the author's suggestion for handling a 401(k) after leaving a job?

    B. Explore options for managing taxes strategically, rather than defaulting to traditional advice.

48. What is the author's view on the need for financial advisors?

    B. Individuals can become their own financial advisors by educating themselves and taking control of their finances.

49. Why does the author criticize the statement, "You will own nothing and be happy"?

    E. All the above.

50. Why does the author believe that people should "own stuff"?

    B. You'll be happier.

Index

About the Authors

MARK QUANN

Mark Quann, known as "Money Mark" for his lifelong fascination with finances, is the founder and CEO of The Perfect Portfolio, a division of REMii Group, Inc. Raised in a blue-collar family with a brick mason father and a stay-at-home mom, Mark knows firsthand the challenges ordinary Americans face when it comes to building wealth. After navigating his way through credit card debt, student loans, and years of financial lessons learned the hard way, Mark unlocked the strategies the ultra-wealthy use to grow their fortunes and reduce taxes—legally.

As a #1 best-selling author of *Top 25 Ways an IUL Can Secure Your Financial Future*, and the author of *Top 10 Ways to Avoid Taxes* and *Rich Man, Poor Bank*, Mark has spent the last four years helping hundreds of families master the same Buy, Borrow, Die strategy used by billionaires to build wealth and pay little-to-no taxes. His mission is simple: to prove that ordinary Americans can use these powerful strategies to take control of their financial future and keep more of what they earn. Based in Knoxville, Tennessee, Mark is committed to teaching people of all income levels how to use the tax code to their advantage, just like the wealthy do.

A.J. MERRIFIELD

A.J. Merrifield is the cofounder and COO of REMii Group Inc., cocreator of The Perfect Portfolio, and coauthor of *Be Smart Pay Zero Taxes*. Formerly a Senior Executive VP at Xerox, Logistics Manager at Amazon, and Finance Director for a network of Harley-Davidson dealerships, A.J. is proof you can go from boardrooms to bikes with ease. A disabled combat Veteran of the US Army with multiple deployments to Iraq, he's now on a mission to help you keep more of your money—because Uncle Sam has taken enough.